This book is an excellent catalyst for any leader to make better decisions and realize your intentions and goals sooner. Mark has done a great job in creating practical and actionable tools to help you unlock and master your 'business mind.' Read Activators *to become the leader you envision!*

SHANNON SUSKO
Serial Entrepreneur, Strategic Execution Expert,
Best Selling Author – *The Metronome Effect* and *3HAG WAY*,
CEO Coach

Activators *is both practical and thought-provoking. Green not only shows how leaders can get more done but why we might be struggling in the first place. A clever combination of science and business that really gets you thinking and ready to take action.*

HAZEL JACKSON
CEO, Biz Group, United Arab Emi

D1473107

Buy this book now. Read the fu.... .....,, ,.~ .,, ., ...leep tonight. If you are not compelled to take action immediately, you will sacrifice your potential to grow and make a greater impact. In that case, give Activators *to friend or colleague who—unlike you —is truly open-minded and hungry to learn!*

Activators *is provocatively positive for anyone committed to making a difference through their leadership. Mark's principles, tools, and thought processes have made a vital difference to my work with leaders and high-performing teams around the world.*

PAUL O'KELLY
founder, paulokelly.com and O'KellySutton,
partner at Kennedy Insights, Ireland

Over the past nine years, I have observed and gotten to know Mark as his coach, mentor, and fellow teacher. Today, due to his experience, growth, and success, he is now my mentor, teacher, and coach. The work of Activators *comes from rigorous research blended with Mark's personal experience, success, and direct observations of why and how CEOs succeed or fail.* Activators *is a key work for all CEOs to digest, implement, and internalize.*

KEITH CUPP
CEO, Gravitas Impact (formerly Gazelles International)

There's plenty of 'what to do' and 'how to do it' leadership content out there, yet very little about 'why' things don't get done. Activators *unearths the invisible mechanisms of underperformance—our unconscious fears, habits, and beliefs—that hold us back. Don't think this applies to you? Think again, then use these practical and effective tools to get out of your own way.*

KEVIN LAWRENCE
author of *Your Oxygen Mask First,* advisor to CEOs and executive teams, speaker

With Activators, *Mark has identified a clear pathway for CEOs to truly become the leaders they hope to be.*

BRAD GILES
founder Evolution Partners and author of *The 5 Roles of a CEO,* Australia

Identical to his coaching style, Mark mixes his vast knowledge of business strategies with a sophisticated understanding of human psychology into a winning recipe for success. Activators *will help you overcome the unconscious mechanisms that cause each of us as leaders to underperform.*

RYAN SASSON
CEO, Strategic Financial Solutions

Mark's success in helping companies go from 'ordinary' to 'extraordinary' lies in a solid process he has laid out in Activators. *Everybody has a few of the pieces to the puzzle, but we struggle to achieve our aspiration from our perspiration. Mark's process bridges those missing gaps and allows you to not only scale your business but to do it more profitably!*

GREG CRABTREE
author of *Simple Numbers, Straight Talk, Big Profits*

Mark has touched a nerve in all of us. We know what we need to do and how to do it, but we're just not getting it done. He makes us dig deep to figure out why. Activators *is practical, with useful tools that will absolutely improve your decision-making and execution, both professionally and personally.*

JILL BELCONIS
CEO, Jill Belconis Enterprises, YPO International Chairman 2010–11

Activators *will challenge assumptions you have made about yourself and what you can accomplish. Only read it if you have a serious thirst for learning and growth, as this book will reframe some of your precon-ceived notions about what it means to be successful in your own life. A great read with impactful tools for personal and professional growth.*

BRANDON DEMPSEY
partner, goBRANDgo

The tools in Activators *will put your mind at ease. Mark breaks down hard and complicated decisions in a simple way that can be life-changing. You know what to do and what is best for your company. Through* Activators, *Mark will help you get there and bring it home.*

CHRISTIAN D. GIORDANO
president, Mancini-Duffy Architecture + Design

We often fall short of what we want to achieve or don't act in a way we know is best, sabotaging ourselves and our organizations. In Activators, Mark describes how our motivators, beliefs, and habits contribute to our own limitations and frustrations and then provides ways to overcome these unconscious mechanisms that hold us back. Mark is one of the leading business coaches in the world today, and the practical tools he shares in the book have proven results in helping CEOs become the leaders they envisioned themselves to be.

GRAHAM MITCHELL
CEO, GROW, South Africa

As our coach for the past four years, Mark transformed our thinking and our ability to perform as leaders. We have grown and, as a direct result, the business has grown. Much of what he's taught us is wrapped up neatly in Activators. Don't think this is just for CEOs; your entire leadership team should read this book.

DAVID SCHNURMAN
CEO, Lawline, Entrepreneurs Organization New York
President 2018–19

One of the biggest challenges our clients face is the fear associated with making a change they 'know' they should make, but keep putting off. Mark's book and system is my guide for helping them face their fears, get really clear about what they want, and make the changes happen so they can get back to growing their business and personal freedom which is our mission at FreeScale. The process in Activators works for all sizes and types of companies while being easy to learn and durable. Simply put, it just works!

RICHARD MANDERS
co-founder, FreeScale Coaching Systems

Mark Green, himself an inspiring model of Activators, *addresses the fundamentals that all CEOs need to excel in both personal and professional growth. This book is a straightforward guide, with easy and effective tools to maximize your potential and have a powerful impact on your life and on those around you. What more could you possibly want?*

CLEO MAHEUX
Sr GI Coaches, translator and publisher of the French edition of
Scaling-Up

I successfully applied many of the concepts described in Activators *twice—as CEO of a large multinational business and then as CEO of a mid-market high-growth firm. Mark's principles work because he enables leaders to focus on the blind spots in their minds that they cannot see.*

BORIS LEVIN
CEO, Mott Corporation

There are a great variety of tools available for people leading scaling up companies, but they all lack one thing: a willingness to ask the question 'what truly holds us back?' Activators *provides the answers to this question along with very practical tools to make your thinking clearer and more productive.*

PIETER VAN OSCH
founder and CEO, Scale Up Company, Netherlands

Activators *provides a set of practical, easy-to-use tools that allow you to think more clearly, unleashing your mindset, and therefore your results.*

RONY ZAGURSKY
CEO, Adaptable—Coaching Your Experience, Mexico

Having had the great pleasure of being mentored by Mark, I am deeply impressed with how well Activators *captures his rich and comprehensive experience. Mark's coaching helped me put many of the eight* Activators *into practice, and they were game changers for my business. Genuine, thoughtful, and easy to follow,* Activators *encompasses Mark's ability to unleash potential in others—as if you're sitting in the same room talking together! You will find simple and effective guidance that will spark the next level of your personal and professional growth.*

MICHELLE LAVALLEE
international talent advisor and certified Topgrading coach, Chile/China

ACTIVATORS

ACTIVATORS

A CEO'S GUIDE TO CLEARER THINKING AND GETTING THINGS DONE

MARK E. GREEN

Printed in the United States of America.
Library of Congress Control Number: 2018956179
ISBN Paperback: 978-1-949639-09-4
ISBN eBook: 978-1-949639-10-0

To my father, Herbert L. Green. He cared deeply about people, gave of himself to serve others, demonstrated a freakish tenacity to figure just about anything out, and kept us all laughing. His memory is a blessing to me every day.

TABLE OF CONTENTS

SECTION ONE
Observe Your Inner Voices

What Do You Really Want?
(And What Are You Willing to Do about It?)

How We Think Leadership Works, and How It Actually Works

SECTION TWO
Understand Your Inner Voices

Motivators Part I: Fear

Motivators Part II: Inspiration

SECTION THREE

Master Your Inner Voices

ACKNOWLEDGMENTS

MENTORS AND COACHES

You cannot arrive anywhere in life without first laying the groundwork to get there. It's been invaluable to have gifted mentors and coaches throughout my career who contributed to my learning, growth, and development, and who set significant stones along my path. With great appreciation, their names and most notable contributions follow in chronological order:

- **MARION SURO** – Marion is a consummate bar-raiser. She challenged me to expect exponentially more from myself and from others and provided the inspiration for my model of accountability.

- **ROY SANDERS** – Roy is the embodiment of unassuming confidence. By example, he taught me more about self-worth and setting boundaries than he could ever realize while simultaneously imparting the finer points of selling and negotiating.

- **DAVID HERDLINGER** – David is the coach's coach. He opened my eyes to the true power of questions and helped me uncover my life's purpose.

- **VERNE HARNISH** – Verne is a master curator and communicator. His book, *Mastering the Rockefeller Habits*, and the professional ecosystem he created enabled significant changes to my coaching practice in 2009. That inflection point has led to more impact and abundance than I could have ever imagined.

- **KEITH CUPP** – Keith is the epitome of values-based servant leadership. By example, he's taught (and continues to teach) me to hold my principles tightly, to build deeper, meaningful relationships, and to more deliberately enjoy life's journey.

- **SHANNON SUSKO** – Shannon is of the rarest breed: she's a brilliant strategist, a master at execution, and a wonderful human being. Her thinking, leadership, generosity, and collaboration inspire me, make me a better coach, and multiply my impact.

THE *ACTIVATORS* TEAM

The path to completing this book required the thinking, collaboration, and directed actions of many significant people. A huge thank you, in alphabetical order, to:

- Jill Belconis, Keith Cupp, Brandon Dempsey, Omar Hikal, Hazel Jackson, Matt Kuttler, Kevin Lawrence, Paul O'Kelly, and Pieter Van Osch, for your key ideas, input, and feedback.

- Ariel Hubbard and the team at Business Ghost, Cynthia Lay, and Sabrina Osborne for your leadership and contributions to the writing, graphics, editing, publishing, and marketing of *Activators*.

- The multitude of brilliant, insightful thought leaders, researchers, and authors referenced throughout the book.

PROFESSIONAL NEIGHBORHOOD

I am abundantly grateful for my professional neighborhood. Many thanks and much appreciation to my clients and to my worldwide network whose curiosity, engagement, support, and encouragement keep me focused, accountable, strong, and growing. They are, in alphabetical order:

- **CLIENTS** – Mary Buletza, Andrew Fisher, Christian Giordano, Robert Herzog, Katie Lemire, Boris Levin, James Mansfield, Yann de Rochefort, Dan Ryan, Ben Saltzman, Ryan Sasson, David Schnurman, Nik Tarascio, Ray Torella, David Weingard, and Ken Wolf

- **COLLEAGUES** – Jill Belconis, Jennifer Walzer Berkowitz, Cheryl Biron, Mike Carroll, David Chavez, Ralph Chromik, Keith Cupp, Brandon Dempsey Sean Evans, Robert Fish, Jerry Fons, Brad Giles, Mike Goldman, Omar Hikal, Ron Huntington, Hazel Jackson, Ian Judson, Kris Kaplan, Paul O'Kelly, Matt Kuttler, Nikolai Ladanyi, Michelle LaVallee, Kevin Lawrence, Cléo Maheux, Rich Manders, Mike Mirau, Graham Mitchell, Jay Niblick, Aquiles Nunez, Craig Overmyer, Jeff Redmon, David Rendall, Les Rubenovitch, Shannon Susko, Ken Thiessen, Carmine Torella, Keith Upkes, Kristine Van Iderstine, Pieter Van Osch, and Rony Zagursky

FAMILY

A special, loving salute to my family—Mom and Dad (to whom I've dedicated this book), Ron and Carolyn Green, Eric and Lindsey Green, and Stephanie Green. You've supported me, cheered for me, celebrated with me, and helped me overcome challenges along the way.

Most of all, I appreciate my wife Keri and my three sons, Bailey,

Jordan, and Casey. I love you tons, cherish our adventures, and laugh so much my face hurts!

Last, but certainly not least, I also acknowledge the many other brilliant, accomplished, fun people around the world with whom I've had the privilege of working over the years whose names are too numerous to mention individually. You shaped me as a thinker, as a leader, and as a coach, for which I thank you.

FOREWORD

Mark Green and I first met in Dallas, Texas at an international coaching summit in 2016. I sold my mortgage banking company after being in that business for thirty years and was in transition from CEO to strategic business coach. Although I befriended plenty of accomplished coaches that week who were incredibly impressive, Mark stood out as a generous, purpose-driven straight-shooter.

Over dinner one evening, I listened intently as Mark described how he built his thriving coaching business, what he valued, and why it mattered to him. He was crystal clear about his life's purpose: to unlock human potential. Mark's presence and clarity were inspiring.

Two weeks later, I was delighted to learn that he had asked to become my coaching mentor.

Mark knew I had the skills and experience of a long-term, post-exit CEO, as a YPO (Young Presidents' Organization) member since 1977, and as YPO International Chairman in 2011. None of that mattered to him: his purpose was to unlock more of my potential, not celebrate my past successes. He challenged me from a deeply caring place.

"What's holding you back?"

"Why is this such a challenge?"

"What assumptions are stopping you here?"

"What are you afraid of?"

And much, much more.

He was right. I knew what I needed to do and generally how to do it, but hesitated to get it done. Mark worked with me to unearth my hidden growth killers—the motivators, habits, and beliefs that invisibly hindered my progress. It made sense to me—like I was discovering a critical missing link within myself—as he led me through the steps and tools. I grew rapidly, and my coaching practice grew rapidly too.

As I reflect on my growth and Mark's mentorship, I recall several moments in my career when I wish I could have acted more rapidly with more clarity. One story stands out as a particularly painful and costly example.

In the early 2000s, we pursued a window of opportunity to further expand our nationwide mortgage banking company through Joint Venture (JV) partnerships. Naturally, as CEO, I wanted to take full advantage of this growth opportunity.

Within weeks of acquiring a team of seasoned mortgage professionals through a new JV partnership with a prominent real estate company, I discovered that the vice president leading the team absolutely clashed with our firm's culture. The implications of this situation were unacceptable. I *knew* we needed leaders who were aligned with our core values. I *knew* we needed to exit her from the business. I *knew* exactly what steps I needed to take to resolve the situation. And yet, I didn't act.

I feared that the owner of the partner firm would side with the team leader and terminate our partnership. I feared that the partner firm would tell our other JV partners that we were the problem, potentially raising concerns with our other successful ventures. These fears dominated my thoughts and paralyzed my leadership.

Unsurprisingly, the situation worsened and eventually ended poorly.

I've observed this same pattern in businesses of all types and sizes, literally all over the world: smart, successful CEOs who *know* what to do or what decision to make, but don't act accordingly. Fear isn't the only issue. It's often unproductive leadership habits, that nagging "voice in your head," and more. These habits and thoughts inevitably lead to cloudy thinking, suboptimal decision-making and delayed critical action.

To my knowledge, Mark's thinking and the content of this book represent the first time anyone has tackled this highly intangible, yet exceptionally costly subject.

Activators is rigorous and research-based, yet accessible and practical. Inside, you'll find a deep exploration of each hidden growth killer and easy-to-use assessments and tools to illuminate your barriers and then reveal the right path forward.

As you'll learn, Mark deliberately surrounds himself with better, smarter, and more experienced people who challenge him, make him uncomfortable, and help him continually grow. Through *Activators*, he will play that role for you—questioning your habits, challenging your deepest thoughts and assumptions, and stretching you—with the ultimate goal of helping you unlock more of your potential as a business leader.

Welcome to the best investment you could ever make—to grow yourself, to scale your business, and to accelerate the legacy you aspire to create.

Jill Belconis
CEO, Jill Belconis Enterprises
YPO International Chairman 2010-2011

INVITATION

Why is it so difficult to execute what I already know I should be doing?

I've witnessed CEOs at all levels of experience struggle with this question in themselves and in others throughout their businesses. It doesn't arise from lack of knowledge or skills; they and their teams generally know what to do and how to get it done. It's also not for lack of information; there is an abundance of "what" and "how" advice out there, which they—and you—have likely consumed in a variety of forms.

But, as you know, what matters is not what you know or what you intend to do—it's what you actually enact. While that statement seems rather obvious, the question above remains. As a veteran coach of high performers, I've seen every one of my clients struggle with this issue. I've seen it cripple coaches I've mentored—I've even faced the same challenge myself. We were all avoiding the decisions, choices, and actions we knew could advance our success. But what was holding us back? And how could we overcome it?

I knew there had to be a solution, and I set out to find it.

I dove into neuroscientific research, behavioral studies, and social science and uncovered what I firmly believe to be the source of the issue: there is a huge disconnect between how we *think* leadership works and how it *actually* works.

All roads lead back to your mind. Unconscious forces in our brains inhibit us from acting on what we know. These forces are our motivators, habits, and beliefs, and when you are unaware of them, they act as hidden growth killers and prevent you and your team from enacting what you set out to do. As such, the question is not *whether* this is a problem for you; it's *how much* this problem is affecting your ability to accomplish your goals.

Odds are, these hidden growth killers are negatively impacting you and your business and are affecting your decisions and your actions. And NEWSFLASH: this is not just happening in *your* head. It's happening throughout the entire ecosystem of your company—within the minds of your partners, leadership team, and every employee and customer you have.

Take a moment to ask yourself what all of this is costing you.

Fortunately, my research didn't just identify the source of the problem. By combining the findings with my own observations, I discovered powerful insights to overcome the hidden growth killers—and in the process, unlock more human potential.

Capitalizing on the Pareto Principle, or 80/20 Rule, I synthesized a small fraction of the research out there to create strategies that generate disproportionately large benefits. The easy-to-implement tools and techniques I employ in my coaching practice and will share with you here empower CEOs to become the leaders they aspire to be and more effectively guide their organizations to scale and greater success.

Here are just a few examples of the progress my clients have made using these strategies:

- After more than a decade of building his business, one CEO took a sabbatical for the entire summer—completely disconnecting from his company. While he was away, the team continued to thrive without skipping a beat, and the business continued to grow.

- One CEO overcame her paralyzing fear and terminated a key executive who was limiting the organization's ability to grow. The very next day, she had a line of employees waiting outside her door to thank her.

- Another CEO was so reluctant to increase prices for his service-based business that he hadn't done so in eight years. After we addressed the fears holding him back, he implemented a 20 percent across-the-board price increase. Every client accepted the new rates without hesitation.

This is not a beginners' guide to effective leadership. Rather, this book builds on your already-strong leadership capacity, merging data, insights, and practical experience into an operations manual for your "business mind." Here, you'll gain insight and acquire tools to get out of your own way, make better decisions, and *fully enact your intentions*. A companion to all the books, conferences, training programs, and people who have taught you the "what to do" and "how to do it" necessary to run your organization, this guide will enable you to execute and get things done. It will help you further elevate into the leader you envision yourself becoming.

The principles, strategies, and tools I'll introduce are universal; they've been implemented with profound impact on businesses in North America, Central America, South America, Europe, and Asia. Further, they apply to companies big and small and are effective regardless of your knowledge and experience level, industry, market, culture, or location.

Read on, and you will unlock your ability to do the following:

- Think with clarity and a sense of purpose.

- Act on what you know you and your team need to do.

- Control the impact of fear on your decisions and actions.

- Replace people around you who are holding you back.

- Become the leader you envision, rather than the person you feel you are right now.

In the coming pages, I will share with you the way our brains work for and against us. I will define eight **Activators**—principles and techniques to clarify your thinking and accomplish more—to help you observe, understand, and master the mechanisms of your mind.

You'll also find an actionable tool corresponding to each Activator to help you master your business mind. Once we've covered the research, examples, tools, and techniques, we'll integrate the findings to transform your sense of purpose, your commitments, and your ability to take action for the better. All of the tools and self-assessments in the book are available for download at www.activators. biz, so you can use them freely and share them with your team.

Throughout this process, you'll reduce the impact of fear, unlock more capability, accelerate growth, and advance toward the freedom, abundance, and legacy you desire for yourself and for those you serve.

Observe Your Inner Voices

What Do You Really Want? (And What Are You Willing to Do about It?)

I t was mid-afternoon on a crisp, cool, fall day in the leafy suburb of Chappaqua, New York, just about an hour north of New York City. I grew up there, in a modest 1960s-era four-bedroom split-level—white with blue shutters—at the end of a quiet street. That day, October 10, 2000, the house was filled to the brim with family and friends.

There was a catered spread in the dining room, a buffet stretching from wall to wall. The aroma of Italian food—garlic, freshly baked bread, and sauced pasta—wafted through the house.

People were talking loudly, with their hands. There were aunts, uncles, grandkids, friends new and old—people from all corners of my life. I couldn't walk three feet without running into someone wanting to check in and catch up. The ebb and flow of conversation made it seem like someone was playing with the volume control; sometimes I couldn't hear myself think. Other moments were almost too quiet.

We buried my father that morning.

"Can you tell us about your father?" one of my friends asked as we stood near the front door. "What was he like?"

I drew in a breath, thinking about how to respond to what felt like a profound question, especially now that I would be answering in the past tense. But before I could respond, the doorbell rang.

"Excuse me," I said, turning to answer it.

A man in a UPS uniform was standing outside. He wasn't toting a package, nor did he have a piece of technology—not even a notepad or a pen.

"Hi," he said, visibly unsure of what to do with his hands. "I just wanted to let you know that I'm very, very sorry to hear about your father. He was really special."

I was completely caught off guard. "I . . . thank you," I stammered.

"He always asked me how I was doing. Invited me in to warm up with a hot cup of coffee in the winter or to cool off with a glass of water in the summer." The man had been staring at his empty hands, but now he looked me right in the eye. "Nobody does that. Nobody does those things. Your father did those things. It meant a lot."

I swallowed hard. I shook his hand. I thanked him, then added, "Please come inside and join us. My father would be so happy to know you stopped by."

He politely declined and went on his way.

As I turned around to face my friends, I realized they had overheard the entire exchange. Tears were running down my face. "That's who my father was," I managed to choke out. "That's what he was like."

LEGACY

My father gave of himself. He comforted and served others. To his friends, to his family, to the man who delivered his packages, he was known as someone who cared deeply.

That is his legacy.

Each of us has a vision, a sense of what we want to create in this life—of what we want our legacy to be.

Take a minute to close your eyes and think about it. What do you want to contribute? How do you want to be remembered?

Fulfilling your vision and achieving the freedom, abundance, and legacy you desire require that you live your life on your own terms. Whether your goal is to make an impact with an industry-disrupting idea, a far-reaching business model, simple kindness—as my dad did—or all three, the journey is as important as the outcome.

But here's the problem: the path and the outcomes that we imagine for ourselves form an idealized picture, one that is often inconsistent with where we feel we are right now.

THE DUALITY GAP: ASPIRATION VERSUS SELF-PERCEPTION

Your ideal self may be a business superhero, a difference maker for people in need, or a CEO building a revolutionary company brick by brick, and yet there are days when you can't fix a simple problem, or you feel more like an amateur than a fearless leader. Experiences like these throw into question the notion that you have it all together, leaving you with the sense that everything could be falling apart. We all have moments that remind us of the duality of how we envision our future versus where we feel we are in the present:

- You aspire to succeed, yet you feel like a failure.

- You aspire to be cool under pressure, yet you feel a lack of control.

- You aspire to be clear-headed, yet you feel indecisive.

- You aspire to be happy, yet you are full of anxiety and worry.

- You aspire to be an amazing spouse or parent, yet you work too much.

DUALITY GAP

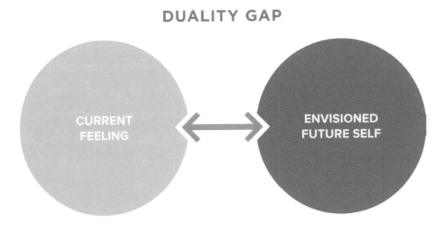

The curated life-illusion of social media fuels the disparity between the aspirational version of ourselves and the person we see in the mirror. No matter what channel you're looking at—LinkedIn, Twitter, Facebook, Instagram—you're getting others' filtered, Photoshopped highlights of the week and likely comparing them to the flubs and false starts that are a natural part of every true achiever's day-to-day existence.

At its core, this disparity is an issue of integrity, or wholeness. We aim to be one way, and yet we feel another. Because we operate in a culture in which we've been conditioned not to admit our very human insecurities—our vulnerability, weakness, and uncertainty—

this dissonance is inevitable. Worse, it exacts a toll. Psychologists call the price we pay for this *emotional labor*.

For instance, if you aspire to be a leading CEO who dominates your field, but you actually feel like a used-car salesman as you scramble to raise funds and build partnerships, getting through a meeting is guaranteed to be draining. And more important, your focus on projecting a superior persona diverts your attention from your interaction with the individual in front of you. It's exhausting, it's unsustainable, and it's certainly not scalable.

The problem is that the person you believe you are today is the one dictating your thoughts, habits, and beliefs—the unconscious forces that affect all of your decisions. That's the person driving your bus. When you are unsure of yourself and your abilities, you're likely to head in the wrong direction, often with the wrong people on board.

PLAYING TO PLAY VERSUS PLAYING TO WIN

Consider what it takes to play a competitive sport: hours upon hours of mental and physical training, a good diet, strategy, and discipline. You must make the decisions and plays necessary to win the game.

If you haven't prepared, if you haven't conditioned your body and mind or made deliberate, informed choices about how you'll play the game, when it's time to take action, you're not playing to win. You're playing to play.

Maybe you feel out of your depth while meeting with a prospective client, or you imagine that you don't belong in the room in the first place—that mindset makes it so you're just happy to be there. For instance, the first time I was appointed to an advisory board, I believed all the other members had far more to contribute in the form of knowledge and experience than I did. I was just glad I had made it through the door. As such, my action-driven approach went out the window, and I couldn't be effective in my new role.

Most CEOs want to play to win, but they let their self-perception affect their choices, and consequently, their heads aren't really in the game. Fearing the consequences of their actions, they avoid doing the things they know they should—like committing to a clear strategy, firing a toxic or low-performing employee, or listening to customers—and limit their potential as a result.

This is where the work needs to be done. It's not about what to do and how to do it; we've established that you already know that part. It's about addressing the issues in your mind so that you can play to win. We'll do that here.

The strategies and tools in this book will help you close your duality gap and better unify the person you think you are at any given moment with the person you aspire to be. As a result, you'll feel in flow more often, be able to tap into your greatest potential, find freedom and abundance in your work and elsewhere, and build the legacy you envision.

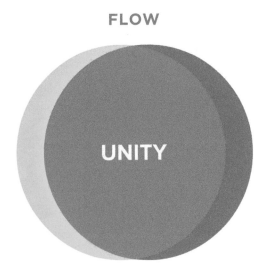

FLOW

UNITY

But first, you have to ask yourself what you're willing to do to make that happen.

THE PRICE OF FREEDOM, ABUNDANCE, AND A LEGACY

This is a marathon, not a sprint. You must put in the work in order to make it to the finish line. The process will require you to stretch. It will demand that you think differently, see things you haven't seen before, ask difficult questions of yourself, and admit things that you haven't previously been able to admit.

Discomfort is part of the process. You don't finish a marathon then head to the gym. You feel pride in your accomplishment, but you're definitely uncomfortable—it's time for a break.

Pushing past the boundaries of your comfort zone is the price I'm asking you to pay for authenticity in lieu of duality, for the freedom and abundance that come from living the life you want to live while building your ultimate legacy.

If you're not interested in stretching, this book is probably not for you. Here's why: *I have never observed a business in which the sustained growth rate of the company exceeded the personal growth rate of the people running it.*

Your growth is essential to this process; if you want to see your company progress, you have to be willing to invest the time and energy necessary to address your personal development.

But if you're ready to do the work, to get closer to the person you aspire to be, and to reap the many benefits of this process, then keep reading. We've got work to do.

KEY TAKEAWAYS

- We all have an idealized version of ourselves that often differs from who we believe we are in the present moment. That disparity undermines our integrity and hinders our ability to achieve freedom, abundance, and the legacy we envision.

- Our choices are directed by the person we think we are. Quite often, that's someone less capable than the leader we imagine. We therefore avoid difficult conversations and tough choices. We choose not to act out of fear. We limit our risks, and thereby limit our potential.

- To unlock our fullest potential, we must close our duality gap by reconciling the person we wish to be with the person we think we are at any given moment.

- Doing so requires us to stretch well beyond our comfort zone. It won't be easy, but it will be worth the effort.

CHAPTER 2

How We Think Leadership Works, and How It Actually Works

Let's pause for a moment. I want you to take thirty seconds to close your eyes and just observe where your mind goes.

. . .

Done? Great. What did you notice? Did you have just one thought or many? Were you focused on a single concept, or did your brain flit from topic to topic? Perhaps your mental chatter sounded something like this:

"Why is he having me do this? I hate when books make me do stuff like this."

"It feels a little cold in here."

"I forgot to return that call!"

"I hear a dog barking."

"I have that early meeting tomorrow; I need to make sure to get out of the house on time."

"What's for dinner tonight?"

"Wow, what an ugly tie."

"That waitress is about to spill soup on that guy."

Everything you observed—every thought that came through—was generated by the voice in your head, the internal narrator we all have. At any moment, this private dialogue runs as background chatter separate from whatever is happening in your real world. Ninety-nine percent of the time, it's unconscious: you don't even realize two narratives are occurring simultaneously. That makes the voice in your head hard to manage.

Here we run into the duality gap discussed in chapter 1: you may know you need to deal with a particular issue in your company, but the voice in your head is doing its best to dissuade you. For instance, you have to talk to an employee about his tendency to hijack meetings and alienate others—but the inner voice counsels timidity: "He's my most valuable employee, and if I piss him off, maybe he'll sell a little bit less, or maybe he'll find another job, or maybe he'll get angry and start disrupting the business in other areas."

The voice can also be your harshest critic, making you feel ill-equipped to handle a particular situation.

But you are not the voice in your head. Rather, as our thirty-second exercise demonstrated, you are just its observer. Though it may be challenging at first, you have the ability to listen to the voice in your head and recognize it as a separate entity. When you're conscious of the chatter, you can control it. And controlling the voice in your head is essential to making sound decisions—and following through with the right action—in business and beyond.

As neurologist, psychiatrist, and Holocaust survivor Victor Frankl so lucidly stated in his book *Man's Search for Meaning,* "Forces beyond your control can take away everything you possess except one thing: your freedom to choose how you will respond to the situation."

TWO SPONSORING THOUGHTS

Here is a basic, practical explanation of human behavior: *every thought we have and every action we take is motivated by the desire to get more of something "good" or less of something "bad."*

These are the two sponsoring thoughts at the root of all behavior; we'll call them love and fear. The "good"—love—includes thoughts about expansion, abundance, growth, and possibility. The "bad"—fear—encompasses anxieties about contraction and scarcity and the urge to protect ourselves.

Fear and love drive all our behaviors. For instance, you may choose to go on a diet because you fear that your partner doesn't find you attractive anymore, or your reason may be love-driven: you want to live long enough to know your great-grandchildren.

We see the impact of these sponsoring thoughts on business decisions all the time: did you fire that volatile employee because you feared what might happen if he stayed on, or did you do it with an eye toward love—expansion and possibility in this case—the ability of the organization to achieve a healthier culture?

While acting out of love (we'll refer to this as "inspiration" in the business context from here on) is the superior option, inspiration-driven decisions often require a willingness to forego short-term rewards in exchange for long-term benefits—and humans have a maddening propensity to repeatedly and deliberately do the opposite. There is ample research on this topic, most notably from Daniel Kahneman who—in his book *Thinking, Fast and Slow*—explains the distinction between System 1 and System 2 thinking, with many clear examples. Why do people continue to smoke cigarettes when they are indisputably terrible for them? Because the perceived short-term social or nicotine-fueled physical rewards of smoking a cigarette eclipse the risk of lung cancer or coronary artery disease twenty, thirty, or fifty years down the road.

It's also why, in business, for example, we are inclined to hire Mr. Right Now as opposed to Mr. Right. We are seduced by the reward of the immediate goal—filling the position, reducing our stress, etc.—and therefore take action despite the inevitable long-term consequence: managing the cost, mess, and recovery from a mis-hire.

Let's take a closer look at how this plays out when it comes to leadership.

HOW LEADERSHIP ACTUALLY WORKS

After years of working with clients, reviewing mountains of research, navigating personal transitions, and just observing people trying to get stuff done, I've come to a sobering conclusion: the way we think leadership works is not how it actually works.

Most of us think the process of leadership looks like this:

1. We *learn* new things, drawing on our experience and other relevant information—or raw inputs—such as our formal education, books, seminars, conferences, mentors, teachers, staff, and peers.

2. We *think* about what we've learned, combine it with available market and competitive data, and engage additional brainpower from coaches, consultants, and economists (or at least their thinking and research). This process seasons and refines the raw inputs from learning and eventually leads us to reach directional conclusions.

3. We use these directional conclusions to *commit* to what we want to do and how to do it—our values, strategy, goals, processes, and the like.

4. We *act* on our commitments through behaviors and processes that embody our core values, maintain accountability, honor

our priorities, and generally support our original vision. The results of our actions provide additional perspective and learning that loops us back to the first step in the cycle.

HOW WE THINK LEADERSHIP WORKS

While the inputs of experience, knowledge, and thinking *do* form a framework within which to commit and act, the next steps are not nearly as straightforward as they seem.

What we don't realize is that before any commitments happen, all that raw material is filtered through three unconscious forces operating in our brains: motivators, habits, and beliefs. These unconscious forces limit our ability to make rational, optimal commitments.

But the interference doesn't end there. After you've made those suboptimal commitments and you're ready to implement your plan, your motivators, habits, and beliefs take their toll *again*. In fact, they are with you every moment of every day and at every step in your leadership journey. This is why business feels really hard, even when you know exactly what to do and how to do it!

HOW LEADERSHIP ACTUALLY WORKS

COMMITMENTS VERSUS CHOICES

Before we proceed, it's important to clarify the difference between commitments and choices.

We'll define *commitments* as big-picture determinants. Fueled by inspiration, they set your business's course. Commitments surrounding core values and core purpose, business strategy, financial structure, policies, and processes are made infrequently, typically at annual or quarterly meetings. While your commitments have a tremendous impact on what you achieve in the long run, they have a relatively low perceived immediate value. None of those things are going to pay you next week, or even next month.

Choices, on the other hand, are tactical day-to-day, hour-to-hour, minute-to-minute selections, usually followed directly by action. The choices that we make and the actions we take today, tomorrow, and next week have a high perceived immediate value and relatively low perceived long-term value. Choices are often fueled by fear: we don't want to lose a customer, so instead of heading in a direction that reflects our core values and our overall strategy, we make a choice—and take (or avoid) an action—that temporarily lets us off the hook. Perhaps we say yes to something unnecessary that helps us avoid conflict today but ultimately limits our overall impact or hurts our longer-term prospects for growth.

We should make choices and take actions that are aligned with our commitments—choices to do the hard, right things—but often we don't. This is where the trouble begins. Our inspiration is easily thwarted by the fear that we won't get paid tomorrow, or that we won't be able to put out the fire burning on our desk. The urge to do something comfortable—something that alleviates fear rather than fuels inspiration—can be overwhelming, and many leaders (all very human) tend to make crummy trade-offs. Instead of focusing on the long game, we get hung up on short-term results and fail to honor our commitments with the right choices and actions. And while our choices may offer quick relief, the fear that drives them creates inertia: the inertia of the comfort zone, of the status quo, and of the quick fix—the swift but limited return associated with fear-fueled action.

FEAR VERSUS INSPIRATION

Some choices are no-brainers: your customer is telling you that if you add a new feature to an existing product—and an easy addition at that—they will place an order today, *and* see themselves continuing to order for the next five years. On top of all that, there seems to be a pretty good market for the new feature.

Then there are those choices that are easy to write off because they involve something with low perceived immediate *and* long-term value; say, a brand-new product request specific to an individual customer who anticipates ordering only once—an item that no one else is likely to want.

It's the middle where we get stuck, where fear and inspiration duke it out.

To overcome the tendency to choose fear over inspiration, you must first be aware of the fact that you are unconsciously motivated to favor fear.

Picture our human ancestor: the early man, millennia ago, standing on the plains of Africa. He hears a rustling in the bushes off to the left. The sound captures his attention instantly. Why? Because it's a matter of survival: that sound could signal the presence of something that will eat him. Or maybe it's just the wind.

Fast-forward to the present: the force of evolution—the process of natural selection—long ago winnowed from the gene pool those who tended to ascribe all such sounds to the wind, and you only had to make that mistake once to get winnowed. Those who survived to pass on their genes *always* responded to that rustling in the bushes as though it were a lion. Of course today we're much less concerned about being eaten for lunch, but that wiring is still there. That's why fear has so much power as a driver of human behavior. It's also why what captures our attention tends to increase in importance to us.

Research has shown that we weigh a negative outcome twice as heavily as a positive one. Studies have reliably demonstrated that when offered the option to take a particular bet, people begin to agree to it only when the potential for gain becomes twice the magnitude of the potential for loss.

The implication of this effect is that to gain ground and take action, we have to raise our inspiration to twice the level of our fear, overriding fear's tendency to hijack our plans. This is where your control of that voice in your head comes in.

WHERE FOCUS GOES, ENERGY AND ATTENTION FLOW

What happens when your iPhone goes *ding*? When your youngest child yells at an older sibling to "Stop it!"? When a familiar face is on the morning news speaking on a topic of interest? These are the kinds of questions social psychologist Robert Cialdini poses in his book *Pre-suasion*.

When a friend tells you that they're shopping for a red car, all of a sudden, you see red cars everywhere. It's not magic; it's a matter of attention. And honing that attention is essential to making the decisions, choices, and actions that best serve your business.

We've all experienced moments of flow—when you're attending to a task that takes all of your concentration. Time slips by unnoticed, you're fully in the zone, and you probably don't notice the voice in your head.

But in the moments right before or after you've applied your fullest concentration—standing at the free-throw line or in a huddle, or in the moments before a business presentation or difficult conversation—the voice is going full tilt. That's when it has to be reined in.

ACTIVATORS

In the early '90s, psychologists K. Anders Ericsson, Ralf Krampe, and Clemens Tesch-Römer set out to determine how people at the very top of their field—true experts—got there. They found that the greatest factor in success was not innate talent but deliberate practice, or "effortful activity designed to optimize improvement."[1]

Deliberate practice requires three things:

- Motivation to stretch one's capabilities

- Extreme repetition

- Flow of feedback

American professional basketball legend Larry Bird would not leave the practice floor until he shot one hundred free throws in a row, of which more than ninety usually went in. This is a perfect example of deliberate practice. He was already at the top of his game, but he insisted on keeping himself in the learning zone. Making ninety-plus of one hundred shots required intense repetition, and from every shot he made or missed he learned something important about his technique.

While this may be an extreme example, it illustrates something vital about your potential: you are not stuck the way you are. You can use specific techniques—or *Activators*—to change the trajectory of your thinking and, therefore, your behavior.

---

1   K. Anders Ericsson, Ralf Krampe, and Clemens Tesch-Römer, "The Role of Deliberate Practice in the Acquisition of Expert Performance," *Psychological Review*, vol. 100, no. 3 (1993), http://projects.ict.usc.edu/itw/gel/EricssonDeliberatePracticePR93.PDF.

IDENTIFYING THE STRUGGLE AND THE SOLUTION

You may be wondering where all of this came from and how I identified the three hidden growth killers and the eight Activators to address and overcome them.

For most of my career, I repeatedly ran into the same kinds of roadblocks and frustrations that hindered and, at times, even derailed my success. I wasn't alone. Over the past decade, I observed that each of my clients experienced similar adversity and friction. Our issues followed a small number of consistent patterns that stemmed from a common set of sources: motivators, habits, and beliefs. Moreover, when I mentioned these observations to my colleagues—veteran business growth coaches from all over the world—they provided reinforcing feedback: they and their clients ran into identical challenges, and virtually all of them were caused by misaligned motivators, habits, and beliefs.

Through learning and experimentation, I determined that these obstacles could almost always be overcome with a handful of strategies—early versions of the Activators and tools we'll employ here. They not only worked for me, but for my clients, for other coaches, and for virtually everyone I knew. Over the years, I found a wealth of evidence in the domains of behavioral research, neuroscience, and social science that further shaped my assertions, bolstered my approach, and enabled a bigger picture to emerge—from which the Activators model, the tools, and this book originated.

As you read Activators, *you'll realize that many of the most frustrating and costly issues you face in business, and in life, arise from the hidden growth killers.* To assess your vulnerability to your motivators, habits, and beliefs, take the Hidden Growth Killer Self-Assessment in the appendix of this book or at www.activators.biz. This fifty-question assessment pinpoints the debilitating behavioral symptoms that my coaching colleagues and I have consistently observed in business leaders running organizations of all sizes across industries, cultures, and geographies. The results will reflect how significantly the hidden growth killers may be affecting your ability to lead your organization.

Armed with knowledge about where your invisible limitations lie and concrete tools to overcome them, you can control your motivators, habits, and beliefs, enabling more productive decision-making, choices, and actions.

We'll begin by developing a better understanding of human motivation.

- You have a constant internal narrator—the voice in your head. But the voice is not you, and when you recognize that it is a separate entity, you can control it. And you *must* do so in order to think and behave more deliberately in business and beyond.

- All of our thoughts and actions are motivated by either inspiration or fear. Thoughts and actions fueled by inspiration tend to have low perceived short-term payoffs and high long-term payoffs, while those driven by fear yield the opposite. Humans are far more likely to trade long-term benefits for short-term gain—often to our detriment. We are usually blind to this.

- While we imagine leadership to be a straightforward process in which we draw on a variety of inputs to make commitments, execute on them, and then learn from the results, unconscious factors—our motivators, habits, and beliefs—intervene at every step.

- Our tendency to make choices fueled by fear undermines our decisions—big-picture determinations that set the business's direction. In order to maintain our integrity and achieve our goals, we have to overcome this tendency.

- The good news is it's possible: by controlling the voice in your head, you can become significantly more effective as a leader.

- Many of the most frustrating and costly issues you face arise from the hidden growth killers. To assess your vulnerability, take the Hidden Growth Killer Self-Assessment in the appendix of this book or at www.activators.biz.

Understand Your Inner Voices

CHAPTER 3

Motivators Part I: Fear

L et's rejoin our human ancestor for a moment, there on the plain. The tall grass rustles. He's afraid. *Could a lion be the cause?* The fight-or-flight response takes hold: his breathing picks up, his pulse quickens, and vasoconstriction in his extremities shunts more blood toward major muscle groups and vital organs.

Back then, fight-or-flight's chain of physical events helped us capture a meal or avoid becoming one. Though our fears rarely stem from life-and-death situations today, the physical response remains. When an employee walks into your office, demands a raise, and threatens to quit, the fact that you're sitting in a comfortable office rather than standing on the plains of Africa is irrelevant to your body.

Fear affects all of us—and likely more than you think. Acknowledging that the majority of our thoughts and behaviors stem from fear requires no stretch of the imagination, particularly in light of how our brains and biochemistry evolved. Studies show that fear often overtakes the decision-making process, leading individuals to make choices based solely on the *potential* of a catastrophic event, no matter how unlikely.[2] Those decisions are typically safe bets—involving less

---

2   Olivier Chanel and Graciela Chichilnisky, "The Influence of Fear in Decisions: Experimental Evidence," *Journal of Risk and Uncertainty*, vol. 39. no. 3 (2009): 2. Accessed online June 27, 2018.

creativity, less risk, and less change—to make us feel physically and/or psychologically safe and more secure. But you *shouldn't* be comfortable in a growing business. Think about Amazon, 3M, Google, and Danaher (which outperformed the S&P 500 by 1,228 percent over the twenty-year period prior to 2018). These companies encourage active experimentation and creativity—and by the same token, the risk of failure.

To overcome your fears and make the kinds of decisions necessary to narrow the duality gap to your aspirational self, you have to understand exactly what you're afraid of, as well as the implications of your fears—and there are many.

THE BIG THREE: EGO, SCARCITY, AND FAILURE

Most fears arise from concerns about one of three factors: ego, scarcity, or failure.

EGO

Ego is all about the need to judge and compare: *how do I stack up?* It's our psychological immune system; it exists to protect us and our sense of self. As such, our ego works to bolster our self-image—rationalizing and even making excuses or blaming others to help us feel whole. When we're constantly attempting to keep up with others or worrying about what they think of us, we lose sight of our own goals in the process. If your moves are dictated by keeping pace with the competition or a need to be liked, you are either playing to play or playing not to lose.

Like all fears, those that are ego-based reduce risk-taking—you resist taking actions, no matter how necessary or urgent, that you believe might negatively affect someone's opinion of you or your status and position relative to an external comparison.

SCARCITY

Scarcity is the notion that there's never enough. These fears arise from several different places.

The source of scarcity fears is money. We all have complicated personal relationships with money. I've worked with plenty of CEOs who have an irrational fear of looking at their financials. It's almost like they don't want to know. Where does this come from?

Imagine a CEO named Ariel transported back to her childhood dinner table at age ten. "Daddy," she says, "At school, my friend Suzy was talking about her house. How much did we pay for our house?" Daddy looks across the table at Mommy, smiles awkwardly, rakes a fork through his mashed potatoes, and says, "Honey, we don't talk about that at the dinner table."

This scenario has played out at dinner tables all across the globe for centuries, which makes it easier to understand how we grow into adults who are unable to comfortably talk about and engage with money. There's no point during high school, college, or early adulthood when we're similarly reconditioned to be okay with money.

The values with which we were raised—along with our current socioeconomic status—also shape our individual mental models of what constitutes a lot of money. For example, someone might consider spending $2,500 on a fancy large-screen television for their living room to be a massively significant purchase. That conditioning doesn't just disappear when he or she takes on a business leadership role handling a $5 million P&L. Just think about the perspective—if $2,500 is massively significant, what must $5 million feel like?

Fear of Missing Out, or FOMO—a concept popularized by millennials—also correlates to the fear of scarcity. We know that, in business, a narrow and deep strategy pays off a heck of a lot more than one that is wide and shallow, but FOMO leads people to choose the latter.

A CEO operating from fear of scarcity may be unwilling to define an explicit and precise business strategy because she worries that she'll miss out on the opportunities that fall just to the left or to the right of her path. Or she may avoid crisply defining her core customer because she's nervous that she could lose other potential buyers with different characteristics. Both of these scarcity-rooted choices can be fatal.

FAILURE

When we talk about failure here, we're not talking about a new product that didn't do well, a bad hire, or even a bad year—we've all weathered and overcome those challenges. It's the *existential* fear of failure: failure to provide for your family, to have time to do the things you want to do, to place big bets and reap the benefits.

While risk aversion caused by ego is transaction based, risk aversion from fear of existential failure is tied to less-frequent big decisions or commitments. You may be doing fine, but you don't want to take a risk that could make you great, because you fear compromising your current relationships and way of life. If your actions are based on worry about the potential impact of limiting your options, your focus will be too broad—you hang onto multiple strategies, with the thought that if one goes south, you'll have other options. Risk aversion stemming from fear of failure often results in massive inefficiencies, competitive disadvantages, and—ultimately—a slow, steady, increasingly painful reduction in cash flow.

If your ultimate goal is to attain freedom and abundance and to leave a meaningful legacy, it's crucial to understand that ego, scarcity, and failure directly limit your potential: ego is a bottleneck to freedom, scarcity is a bottleneck to abundance, and failure is a bottleneck to leaving your legacy.

If you're constantly comparing yourself to others or have a strong need to be liked, how can you ever be free? You'll always be a prisoner to your perceptions about the thoughts and deeds of others. Fearing scarcity is a self-fulfilling prophecy—worrying about how much you have means that regardless of how much you get, it won't ever be enough. Failure follows the same set of considerations: when you're consumed with avoiding it, you can't possibly take the right kinds of risks and make meaningful progress toward leaving behind the legacy you desire.

SYMPTOMS ASSOCIATED WITH FEAR-BASED DECISION-MAKING

How do you know if your ego-, scarcity-, and failure-based fears are driving your decisions and commitments, and what can you do about this?

Like many interventions, diagnosis starts with you. Check yourself for the five general symptoms associated with fear-based decision-making:

- **A tendency to move away from loss rather than toward gains**. Fear-based decision-making is much more about avoidance than pursuit. For instance, if you're totally focused on stopping customer complaints, preventing shipments from going out late, or keeping your margins from eroding instead of achieving growth targets, then fear is the culprit.

- **Procrastination.** Maybe you're waiting for more data or more clients or more money, but whenever you are delaying a decision, fear is probably preventing you from acting. And when you avoid action, you're sticking with the status quo by default.

- **The flip-flop.** You have a meeting where you come to a particular decision with your team. But later that day, you have lunch with another CEO, who shares a horror story related to what you've just decided.

You question your decision, get back to the office, and send your leadership team an e-mail retracting your decision and replacing it with something else. You're swayed by what others say, by the headlines, or by any number of other factors. Fear fosters a tendency to question, doubt, and change your mind rather than stay the course.

- **Unreasonable continued sacrifice.** You choose to give up potential good things in order to maintain what you have, even if there are significant downsides. Maybe you have a salesperson who produces but doesn't complete their paperwork. You know you should do something, but you need the revenue, so you decide to live with it for now—even though the right new hire would be equally productive *and* fulfill all their responsibilities. It's bird-in-the-hand thinking . . . except the bird is pecking at your face.

- **In your gut, you know you're doing the wrong thing.** The issue with the first four symptoms is that that they're obvious to everyone in your organization. Reality check: there are no secrets in your business. Human beings are terrific at reading behavior and inferring its root cause. In other words, while the bird is pecking at your face, the entire company is watching.

  The last symptom—that feeling in your gut that you're doing the wrong thing—may be less visible to others, but it is one of the clearest signs of fear. Those I coach will often verbalize their internal conflict: they know they need to fire a client, *but* . . . Or they know they need to change their banking relationship, *but* . . . And though they can find ways to justify their actions (or lack thereof), their gut feeling is a strong indicator that those actions are fear-induced.

The duality dilemma shows up here too: *you can't feel like a great CEO when you're not addressing the behaviors that weaken your business.* Worse, your fear-based decision-making reinforces itself. Feeling upset about your inability to address a particular problem fuels rumination, which leads to more fear, and so on.

The physical response associated with fear works as another detrimental feedback mechanism. Your body's reaction serves as justification for your fears; they must be real because you actually *feel* the effects. Then your ego jumps in to judge and compare how you're feeling to how you think you *should* be feeling. See how this can quickly become an energy-sucking, downward spiral?

THE INVISIBILITY CLOAK OF AUTOMATIC THINKING

Here's the real rub: you're either blind to or in denial of the vast majority of your fears and the fear-based decisions you're making. Why?

We use logic to justify our decisions, and this helps to make our fears invisible to us. If you ask any CEO why he made the decision to continue doing business with a customer who presents a number of significant challenges, he'll be able to justify his decision with a strong, logical argument that doesn't begin to capture the reality—he is afraid of what would happen if he ended that relationship. He's not trying to fool you with a web of rational considerations; he is actually unaware that fear, rather than logic, is behind his decision. It's a total blind spot.

This brings us back to psychologist Daniel Kahneman and his work identifying System 1 and System 2 thinking.[3] System 1 thoughts are rapid and automatic: someone drops a plate in a restaurant, and you sit up straight. Or while driving, your foot magically moves to the

---

3   Daniel Kahneman, *Thinking, Fast and Slow* (New York: Farrar, Straus and Giroux, 2011).

brake pedal when you detect motion in your peripheral vision. System 2 thinking is slower and more deliberate—it operates in any situation in which you're carefully weighing options, rewards, and consequences.

Much of our life is governed by System 1 thinking. This is usually a good thing; in most situations, it makes us efficient and can even save our lives (let's not forget our human ancestor, escaping lions by the skin of his teeth and the speed of his adrenaline-driven feet). But there are times—particularly in business—when it does more harm than good.

There are three rule-of-thumb biases ingrained in our System 1 thinking that foster unconscious fear-based decision-making:

- **Anchoring**

  We have a tendency to compare experiences. If your last difficult conversation had a negative outcome, the interaction becomes an anchor—your frame of reference. Anytime another potentially difficult conversation is looming, you'll try to avoid it to prevent a similar exchange.

- **Availability**

  Think of availability as a bias of proximity. If you live in San Francisco, California, you're probably not very concerned about being attacked by an alligator. You don't live near alligators, so they're not readily available to you or to your anxiety.

  However, you may very well worry about the potential for a catastrophic earthquake. Further, if an earthquake recently happened elsewhere, your fear would become more pronounced, at least temporarily—especially if the potential for an earthquake might affect any of your decisions.

  If you've been operating your business in a specific manner for a long time, the model or processes you use are highly available. Without you realizing it, availability stealthily encourages you to discount other options, even if their merits suggest otherwise. Your argument for maintaining the status quo may seem perfectly logical, but that justification is based on your availability bias.

- **Representativeness**

  Representativeness is a bias of categorization. It's a mental shortcut we use, largely to great benefit. If I show you a picture of two men, one tall and fit and the other short and fat, and ask you which one is more likely to be a professional athlete, you won't hesitate to pick the former. But there are disadvantages to lumping things together. We are also readily fooled by appearances and limited-exposure first impressions.

  Overgeneralizing can be limiting. For instance, if you hire people with a certain background because someone with that same background was successful, you're probably forgoing a number of great candidates who could bring a new perspective to the position and to your firm.

ACTIVATOR NUMBER 1  REDUCE FEAR

Fear is the foundation of many of your decisions, and that's okay; it's true for each of us. Until you choose to confront your fears, they're guaranteed to invisibly drive your thinking and behavior.

The good news is that there are a number of techniques and tools you can implement to prevent fear-based decision-making. We'll take a deep dive into how to effectively address your fears at the end of this chapter using the Fear Reduction tool, but for now, let's go over a few techniques you can use to interrupt fear-based decision-making today.

SLOW DOWN

Cultivate System 2 thinking as part of your decision process by slowing down. Consider the example of the employee in your office demanding a raise and threatening to quit. You may feel the urge to act immediately. Don't. Actually, don't even think much about it in that moment.

Rather, ask clarifying questions and request time to mull it over. By slowing down, you avoid the pitfalls of making a knee-jerk, System 1 choice and enable System 2 activation for more logical and less emotional thinking. Taking a deep breath—or any other meaningful pause—overrides your default response and gives your brain the opportunity to slow down.

DON'T BE THE MOST EXPENSIVE HOUSE IN THE NEIGHBORHOOD

In 1993, as I began looking to buy my first house, my grandpa Ben pulled me aside one day and said, "Mark, I need to give you a piece of advice before you buy a home."

"Sure, what's your advice?" I asked.

"No matter what you do, don't ever buy the most expensive house in the neighborhood."

"Why not?" I asked.

"There's only one way the other houses in the neighborhood can affect your property value over time."

I thought momentarily about his advice. It made perfect sense to me, so I thanked him and moved on. When I eventually made that first purchase, I did as he suggested, and to this day, I've heeded his advice in all of my real estate transactions.

It didn't occur to me until about a decade later that my grandpa Ben was not just giving me real estate advice. By then I had established my coaching practice, and I was affiliated with an organization of coaches primarily in the leadership development business. At one of our quarterly meetings, as we sat discussing a topic that had become well-trodden ground for me, I experienced an incredible flash of insight: I had become one of the most expensive houses in my professional neighborhood!

I had more experience and more clients than most members of the organization, and sure enough, my continued participation was decreasing my professional value over time.

From that moment forward, I deliberately surrounded myself with people who are better than me, who make me a little uncomfortable, who challenge me, and who will help me grow. It's the only way for me to continually improve.

One day, in your mastermind group, networking organization, forum, or peer group, you may realize you're contributing a lot but reaping very little. If that's the case, any advice you get from the group will likely embody *their* fears—and potentially validate some of your own—dragging down your value over time.

On the other hand, if you surround yourself with individuals who have already reached the next level—who have broken past the place where you are, they'll be able to help you stretch and challenge you to grow, increasing your value over time.

LAY YOUR CARDS ON THE TABLE

About a year into my relationship with a client in the technology sector, we assessed their employees' performance and cultural fit using a methodology called Topgrading. Through this rigorous process, it became clear that, to fulfill their commitment to continue growing, they would have to make the choice to upgrade some of their staff.

Such an epiphany is not uncommon—it often takes an outside perspective to fully illuminate how and why things should be handled differently. As illustrated in chapter 2, situations that challenge you to align your choices with your commitments tend to go one of three ways:

1. The executive team denies that there is a problem, takes no action, and continues on its way.

2. The team operates inside its comfort zone and takes limited, low-risk actions but stops short of the steps necessary to achieve real results.

3. Team members swallow hard and do everything that needs to be done, exchanging some short-term pain for a significant long-term payoff.

COMMITMENTS AND CHOICES

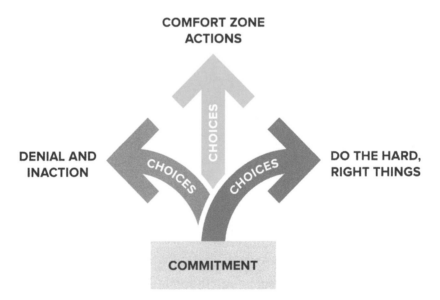

Unbeknownst to these executives, they were standing at this three-pronged fork in the road. The first thing that emerged from our conversation about upgrading staff was fear. They worried about what would happen. Would the terminated staff walk out the door with important institutional knowledge? Would they take other employees or customers with them? Would they bad-mouth the company online?

As we laid everything on the table, the executives realized that their fears were actually limited to a relatively small subset of employees. They also determined that the cost associated with retaining each of those individuals was greater than the fear of what could happen when they were let go.

By engaging in very deliberate, logical, non-emotional thought, the executives reduced their fear and chose the best long-term course of action.

But even that wasn't enough. Remember, in order to truly marginalize fear, your inspiration has to be twice as strong.

TOOL: FEAR REDUCTION

Describe your fear as specifically as possible in the category that applies:

SCARCITY _____

_____

_____

_____

_____

EGO _____

_____

_____

_____

_____

FAILURE _____

_____

_____

_____

_____

Identify the worst-case outcome if you make a commitment.

_____

_____

_____

Are the potential negative outcomes temporary or permanent?

_____

_____

_____

Estimate the _realistic_ probability (expressed as a percent) of this outcome: _____

_____

_____

Name specific previous experiences you've had that support your assessment of the permanence and probability of the worst-case outcome. _____

_____

_____

In the event of your worst-case outcome, how would you recover? Be specific here as well. _____

_____

_____

Name one to three risk areas associated with your commitment. Indicate your perception of the current risk profile on a continuum. Examples:

Price   high risk -----X------------------------ low risk

Testing   more risk ----------------------X------ less risk

_____   ------------------------------

_____   ------------------------------

_____   ------------------------------

How can you reduce the perceived risks associated with your commitment? _____

_____

_____

_____

_____

Discuss the Fear Reduction information above with someone who has no stake in your commitment, like a coach, mentor, forum mate, or peer. Invite them to challenge your thinking.

KEY TAKEAWAYS

- Though fear serves less of an evolutionary purpose than it used to, it invisibly influences the majority of your decision-making.

- You can overcome fear and thus improve decision-making, but doing so requires you to identify your fears and understand their implications.

- In business, our fears are usually tied to ego, scarcity, and (existential) failure. These are direct bottlenecks to freedom, abundance, and your legacy.

- Understanding the symptoms of fear-based decision-making and the rule-of-thumb biases that mask your fears will help you take steps to address them.

- Slow your thinking, surround yourself with more experienced people, and pinpoint exactly what you fear in order to minimize fear's impact on your thinking and behavior.

CHAPTER 4

Motivators Part II: Inspiration

My clients conquered their fears of upgrading their staff. They reviewed their options and determined that the long-term benefits outweighed the potential short-term consequences. They committed. Now they had to elevate their inspiration enough to act—raising it to more than double the level of their fear ($2I > F$).

To do this, we began talking about *aspirations*.

What were their aspirations for the business? For themselves as individuals? Where was the company headed, how did they plan to get there, and how might that process help each individual in the pursuit of their own personal aspirations?

This team was seriously considering a new business strategy and putting stakes in the ground to make it happen. Although this would require them to do business differently, they found it inspiring rather than fear-inducing.

The potential of the plan and the excitement it generated further clarified that staff upgrades were necessary—retaining underperformers would slow or even completely undermine their new strategy.

After our conversation that day, the executive team embarked on a fair but rigorous process to improve the quality of their staff. In the span of one calendar quarter, they terminated 10 percent of their one hundred-plus employees.

Ten percent sounds like a big scary number—after all, they still needed to sell to and serve their customers—but in the end, it was exactly what they needed to do. The process unfolded smoothly, and today they are rebuilding—and advancing—their capabilities with higher-performing players who think, work, and communicate in a manner consistent with their strategy *and* their culture. Even better, the new hires contribute and add value sooner, in more and different ways than the executive team had optimistically anticipated.

They reduced their fear of committing, then increased their inspiration to ensure action.

THE POWER OF PURPOSE

Inspiration is a powerful motivator, and it starts with clarity of vision or purpose and can often be deeply personal—even for business endeavors.

The phrase *life's purpose* may sound a bit touchy-feely, but there's no need to gather crystals or burn incense for this section of the book. There's nothing even slightly fluffy about tapping into a sense of purpose to achieve something important. Hundreds of research studies tell us that big-picture objectives—like impact, one's legacy, and an overarching purpose—are catalysts for inspiration and success-generating actions.

If you think that you still want to tune out here, recognize the voice in your head—the hidden growth killer—pulling you back to the perceived safety of the comfort zone of your habits (we delve into the good, the bad, and the ugly of habits in the next chapter). Defining a purpose can be intimidating because it requires you to push past boundaries and better align your decisions and actions—to truly walk your talk. However, you know by now that staying within the bounds of your comfort zone isn't the path to anywhere other than where you are right now.

We'll work together to clarify your life's purpose later on. Next, we'll discuss how purpose elevates inspiration and directs action.

PURPOSE IN ACTION

Determining purpose—whether in your life, in a business initiative, or even a task—and then applying the rigor, intent, and discipline to live it require a front-loaded investment but pay dividends over the long haul. For additional compelling arguments on the value of a strong purpose, consider reading Simon Sinek's book *Start with Why*.

I first witnessed the power of purpose soon after I launched a leadership development training business in 2003 and affiliated with an organization called Resource Associates Corporation (RAC). RAC created a community of coaches and trainers, and I was there to learn how to facilitate leadership development processes and how to market and build my business. At our quarterly development sessions, I struggled to understand how the more seasoned practitioners solved problems so effortlessly, how they helped new practitioners get to the crux of what they needed to learn, or simply said the difficult thing during difficult conversations. They seemed to be fearless!

In hindsight, what I observed wasn't fearlessness at all. It was *purposefulness!* These experienced leaders cut to the core of an issue, coached others, and said no to the wrong things effortlessly because they had clarity of purpose. While their choices and actions seemed like bold moves, in reality, these leaders expended very little effort; the options in front of them either aligned with their purpose or didn't.

Since then, I've defined my own life's purpose and utilized it to accomplish all manner of things, both personally and professionally. I also model this mindset and associated behaviors for my clients and for the coaches I mentor and train around the world. I know what to say no to, what to say yes to, and how to help others learn to do the same.

When you define your purpose and commit to clarity, decision-making becomes much easier. You rule out anything that doesn't align with your big-picture plan. To quote the late sales guru, motivational speaker, and trainer Zig Ziglar, "Don't become a wandering generality. Be a meaningful specific."

PURPOSE AS A GUIDING PRINCIPLE

I use my life's purpose—to unlock human potential—as a framework to approach every situation, whether it's with my clients, my friends, my kids, or someone I've just met. It's why I'm writing this book. Using purpose as a guiding principle makes day-to-day, hour-to-hour, and moment-to-moment choices easier—and better—for me. I can quickly and easily determine whether taking a particular route serves my purpose and/or my goals—and then act then accordingly.

For instance, one of the things I've learned over the years is that, in order for me to fulfill my purpose and help someone change, he or she has to have the desire to do so. It's about deeds, not words—don't tell me you want to change, show me.

If I detect that I'm more interested in the success of a particular client than he or she is, I have to disengage. I recall a phone conversation several years ago with a CEO who was referred to me as a prospective client. Although the charter jet business she built was successful by any measure, she was in denial of the reality that her leadership style was preventing the business from scaling further. During our conversation, she repeatedly refused to accept any accountability for the conditions in the business that were creating massive stress for her and for her team. I wished her well and ended the call. This may seem cold at first, but deciding to move on allows me to help others who want to be helped and are willing to do the work required, enabling me to have maximum impact and remain true to my purpose.

SHIFTING YOUR YES-TO-NO RATIO

Honoring your life's purpose boils down to making choices and taking actions that promote it—essentially, it's about what you say no to.

Most CEOs I meet maintain the wrong yes-to-no ratio. They commit to far too many things. They also don't realize that delaying a decision is actually saying yes to the process of deciding! This is due in part to FOMO but mostly to lack of purpose. When the target isn't clear, you are likely to aim at anything that moves—usually by saying yes. You believe that agreeing to everything is in your interest. In the moment, that feels like an advancement of something, but in reality, it's like a heavy bucket of sand tied around your neck into which you just dumped another shovel-load. It's slowing you down.

And saying yes to something is effectively saying no to other potentially important things—there are only so many hours in a day, and most resources are finite. This raises the question of whether you are unconsciously saying no to the wrong things. Again, clarity of purpose can show you the way.

You have a yes-to-no ratio whether you realize it or not. It's a simple, easy-to-track key performance indicator (KPI) that you should check periodically to assess the quality of your focus as a leader. Try it for the next full business week by counting all of your yes responses and all of your no responses, and be sure not to miss the stealthy ones—head nods or terms like *sure*, *yeah*, and even *why not*.

Being conscious about your yesses is an important mechanism to get this measure in check. The right yes-to-no ratio is actually much smaller than you think—maybe one yes to every ten nos. Most businesspeople need to reduce their yes-to-no ratio by a factor of about ten! Just think about what you could accomplish if you started saying no more often!

RESETTING YOUR LOCUS OF CONTROL

How much time do you spend thinking about and acting on *your wants*, versus the opinions, interests, or desires of others?

A former client of mine did far more of the latter. He built and ran a highly successful business, and, though he had a capable leadership team who readily offered their insights, the input that swayed him most came from his wife.

He and his team would have a meeting, discuss their desired outcomes, and agree on a course of action. But when the workday ended, his wife would ask him a litany of questions that would cause him to question the decisions he had made. He'd return to the office the next morning and ask his team to reevaluate their determinations or simply overturn them on his own.

Even worse, the CEO's wife wasn't a very trusting person, and she had transplanted her sense of skepticism into him—yet another factor that frustrated his executives. Unfortunately, the CEO was unwilling to fully engage with and address these issues, and as a result, my engagement with him lasted only one year. Soon after, several of the strongest members of his leadership team set out in search of better opportunities.

This is not a story about a family business, nor is it one about marital dynamics. Rather, it illustrates the difference between self-directed and other-directed decisions, choices, and actions. When you don't maintain a strong locus of control, stay the course, and call your own shots, you're saying yes to someone else's plan. And, if you don't have a plan of your own, you are *always* saying yes to someone else's plan.

Lacking a strong locus of control can also derail us personally: being swayed by others' plans and opinions is a massive consumer of dreams and aspirations. There are thousands of would-be chefs and musicians out there who were convinced to be doctors or lawyers instead, and it's not unusual to hear them mention their regrets twenty or thirty years later.

David Klein found himself facing a similar set of circumstances. When David and I first met, he was a practicing attorney working eighty hours per week. He was only an associate at the time, but the partners at his firm were working just as many hours! David's quality of life was dismal, and he couldn't see it getting any better—even if he eventually made partner.

David began thinking about a change of course. He was a licensed private pilot with a true passion for aviation, though he rarely had the opportunity to fly. While many people told him how fantastic it would be to become an attorney, unsurprisingly no one encouraged him to become a professional pilot, and he knew many of his friends, family, and colleagues would be critical if he chose to make the switch. Still, he decided to follow his own locus of control. He quit his job at the law firm and earned his flight instructor certificate.

He began teaching students to fly as a means of acquiring the 1,500 flight hours necessary to work for commercial airlines. Today, David is a full captain working for a leading fractional jet ownership company. He works a total of twenty-one weeks per year—seven days off, seven days on. Not only does he have the kind of flexibility and freedom that he could have only dreamed of as an attorney, but he also loves his work. He flies helicopters now, too, and still teaches as a flight instructor, simply because it brings him joy.

David's decision and subsequent journey are out of the ordinary. I've encountered many CEOs who operate their businesses entirely on externalities. For example, the performance metrics in a business's loan covenant dominate every choice they make. But a bank's goal is to profit from their loans, not to build that CEO's business or provide for her family or fulfill her purpose. There's no self-direction or inspiration there.

Being self-directed means you're getting what you want on your terms, using your own standards to measure progress and accomplishments. In order to do that, *you have to know what you want.*

GOAL SETTING

We've discussed the impact of purpose and its role in fueling inspiration. Now it's time to ask yourself some big questions:

- What is your highest aspiration personally?

- How will you make a positive impact on the world?

- What are you fighting for, and how do you know it's worth it?

- What do you want more of? What do you want less of?

Your answers notwithstanding, *hope is not a plan.* To achieve desired outcomes, you must make choices and perform actions that align with what you want. As Stephen Covey astutely pointed out in his book *The 7 Habits of Highly Effective People*, it is always best to "begin with the end in mind."

Numerous studies have demonstrated the impact of goal setting, particularly its effect on two factors: motivation and achievement. Those with goals are far more likely to achieve them than are people with murkier objectives.

Knowing that 25 percent of students who attend four-year universities never complete their programs—thanks in part to hazy purposes and lack of motivation—clinical psychologist Dominique Morisano and her colleagues set out to determine whether goal setting would improve their performance. It did. After just four months, students who engaged in goal setting displayed significant improvement in both motivation and academic performance compared to those who did not.[4]

Similarly, backward design, an educational model that uses goal setting as the mechanism for lesson creation, guides teachers to identify learning goals before determining their lesson plans. Defining clear finish lines allows them to incorporate achievement into the lessons themselves, and since the late 1990s, research has repeatedly demonstrated the efficacy of this method.

ACTIVATOR NUMBER 2  INCREASE INSPIRATION

Increasing inspiration is an analogous process to reducing fear, and it is of equal importance. Just as my clients determined their worst-case scenario as they went through the process of upgrading their staff, they also thought about the best possible outcome and its corresponding short- and long-term gains. When they thought about the potential of their new business strategy, their inspiration increased enough to activate their commitment. When you believe in what you're doing and where you're headed, you tilt the $2I > F$ equation in your favor and you are much more likely to act.

Clarifying purpose using the Know Your WHY tool described in the next section, evaluating your yes-to-no ratio, and determining whether your business decisions, choices, and actions are self-

---

4   Dominique Morisano et al., "Setting, elaborating, and reflecting on personal goals improves academic performance," *Journal of Applied Psychology*, March 2010, https://scholar.google.com/citations?user=PhOPwWsAAAAJ&hl=en.

directed—and taking steps to change them if they're not—are valuable ways to increase your inspiration.

TOOL: KNOW YOUR WHY

Knowing why something really matters helps you engage your emotions and take action, even in difficult circumstances.

Purposefulness is a chronically underutilized resource, often at great expense! Here again, we find ourselves tending to focus on the what to do and how to do it while lacking clarity on the WHY. Check the voice in your head right now before continuing: hidden growth killers lurk in abundance around the topic of purpose.

Start interacting with this tool by naming a tactical outcome that represents a right choice in alignment with one or more larger commitments: a goal, a target, or perhaps a behavior, habit, or belief that you want to change. Then you'll dig down to the bedrock of purpose—the WHY—through a series of repetitive questions—each deepening the previous answer.

As you progress, try to move from logical answers to deepening emotional answers. I use the "goosebump test." That is, I know I hit the bedrock, emotional WHY when it gives me goosebumps.

This process helps you identify the aspiration or purpose of your objective. When you know your WHY, you will manifest the inspiration necessary to move forward—to act.

What is your goal, or the behavior, habit, or belief that you want to change? _____

_____

_____

_____

ANSWER THESE FIVE WHYS:

Why is that important to you?

_____

_____

_____

Why does that matter?

_____

_____

_____

Why is that important to you?

_____

_____

_____

Why does that matter?

_____

_____

_____

Why is that important to you?

_____

_____

_____

- Clarifying your aspirations and purpose is a catalyst for inspiration—motivating you to act.

- Determining purpose, and then applying the rigor, intent, and discipline necessary to live it requires work up front but pays dividends forever. Using purpose as a guiding principle makes day-to-day, hour-to-hour, and moment-to-moment choices easier—and better.

- Without a defined target or purpose in mind, you say yes to too many things. This habit severely limits your potential. Tracking and then changing your yes-to-no ratio is required to control your time and the journey to your aspirations.

- Many CEOs operate their businesses entirely on externalities. Self-directed people get more of what they want on their own terms. To join them, you must know what you are aiming for. Goal setting can help, increasing both inspiration and achievement.

- Use the Know Your WHY tool to dig to the bedrock of purpose—your emotional WHY. This is the tool to clarify purpose and transactionally tip the $2I > F$ equation in favor of action.

CHAPTER 5
Habits

Like motivators, habits serve an evolutionary purpose. When our ancestors dug for roots and tubers, they didn't have to think through the step-by-step process of excavation each time they touched the soil. Instead, the formation of habits made digging a mindless activity, preserving mental bandwidth for other, more pressing, concerns—like watching for lions.

Habits still serve an important purpose in our lives: they save processing power. You experience the mindless function of habits every day. How many times have you driven to work without giving the trip itself a second thought? From the moment you entered the car to the second you stepped through your office door, you were on autopilot. At no point did you think, "Oh, I need to turn left at the next light, then turn right down there. Ah, I'd better watch out for this merge." And yet, you drove safely and competently, perhaps while considering your schedule for the day or brainstorming a creative solution to a business opportunity, a sales issue, or your child's upcoming birthday party.

While all habits serve a purpose, some are better than others (brushing and flossing each night before bed versus biting your nails or saying *um*, *ah*, or *like* when you speak in public). Habits also profoundly affect our decisions, choices, and actions in business.

Regardless of the ways your habits help or hinder you, they are all formed in the same manner. To get to the root of your habits—good and bad—you need to understand how they form.

HABIT FORMATION

Habits begin simply enough, with a single episode. You eat a cookie when your energy lags at three o'clock, or you pick up a newspaper across the street from your office in the morning. If the outcome of your behavior is positive, pleasing, or productive, the odds are that you will repeat it, and have a cookie or get the newspaper the next day. Over time, repetition makes these behaviors permanent and mindless, separating them from conscious thought. Habits are also formed through exposure alone. This is why you learn annoying marketing jingles, remember every lyric to a decades-old song, and why you may have relationship issues with money, as we discussed in the context of fear earlier. Exposure and repetition are the crucible of how your habits form, why a 3:00 p.m. cookie becomes an everyday indulgence, and why you buy the paper every morning—whether you read it or not.

In his 2012 book *The Power of Habit*, author Charles Duhigg highlights neurological research from MIT in the early 1990s that identified a simple three-step loop that governs the formation and maintenance of habits. A *cue* triggers the habit; then there is the *routine* of the habit itself, which can be physical, mental, or emotional; and finally, there is always a *reward* that reinforces the value of the routine in response to the cue. Over time, this three-step loop of cue, routine, and reward becomes so automatic that we crave the reward at the signal of the cue.[5] In other words, when the clock says 3:00 p.m. (cue) you can taste the cookie (reward) before you even get up

---

5   Charles Duhigg, *The Power of Habit* (New York: Random House, 2012).

from your desk (routine). Change isn't always fast or easy, but when compared to the cost of a bad or counterproductive habit, the path becomes quite compelling.

Picture your habits forming in the same way the deeply grooved wagon-wheel ruts formed on the Oregon Trail in the mid-1800s as fur traders and pioneers traveled from Missouri to settle the western United States. The early wagons made light tracks through the dust on the newly formed trail, but as more and more wagons traversed the route, the ruts became so deep that once wheels entered them, they couldn't get out without major effort. If the settlers only wanted to head due west, the ruts served them—they didn't even have to steer! But what if they chose a different direction, or if they experienced an emergency and had to change course?

That's when they paid the price for those deep ruts.

Your habits are the equivalent of deep wagon-wheel ruts in your mind. Just because a habit serves you in one circumstance, that doesn't mean it will be of benefit in another. If you've ever accidentally driven to work on a Saturday morning when you meant to meet a friend for brunch, you've experienced this in action.

HABITS OF THOUGHT

Habits can be physical—brushing your teeth, tying your shoes, driving to work. Or they can be mental—habits of thought—your attitudes about money, your superstitions, your beliefs, and your expectations of others.

Habits of thinking show up all the time in business. The way we conceptualize luck is a perfect example. Business researcher, consultant, and author Jim Collins explores the concept of return on luck in his book *Great by Choice*.[6] Collins set out to determine whether

---

6   Jim Collins, *Great by Choice* (New York: HarperBusiness, 2011).

higher-performing companies had just experienced more luck than their lower-performing counterparts. To do so, he compared the events experienced by paired companies in the same industry and time frame, one of which was ten times as successful the other. For an event to be considered "lucky" it had to a) occur independently of people's actions; b) have a significant impact on the business, whether positive or negative; and c) have an element of unpredictability.

Collins determined that the higher-performing group did not have more luck than the other. So what accounted for the difference in their success?

He found that the higher-performing companies were able to achieve a better return on their good luck, while lower-performing companies squandered more luck-based opportunities. The inverse was also true: higher-performing companies figured out how to capitalize on bad-luck events—adhering to the philosophy of "what doesn't kill us makes us stronger," while the others did not.

Collins's research demonstrates something I've found while working with my clients over the years—habits of thinking about luck set the stage for the kind of returns companies generate. The way a leader approaches winning a large account will affect the outcome. For instance, he might think to himself, "This is fantastic, we can sit back and relax now; we've achieved some security," and use it as an opportunity to catch his breath. Unfortunately, by leaning back after a big win, he will probably generate a fair to poor return on a good-luck event—and miss the chance to further capitalize on it.

On the other hand, if he were to think, "Wow, we just won this big account. We've got momentum—it's time to double down and create a new sales incentive program to help our salespeople continue to crush it in the market," his approach would likely lead to a much better return on the same event.

Of course, this holds true for the opposite scenario: one's habits of thought create self-pity or directed action in response to a negative event. As we observe in Jim Collins's research, those choices led to widely divergent outcomes over time.

THE PITFALLS OF UNPRODUCTIVE HABITS

While taking the high road may seem like the obvious choice, a number of unconscious mechanisms maintain our less-than-optimal habits and make it hard to break them—or even to realize they exist in the first place.

These are the most common unproductive leadership habits that my colleagues and I observe:

- Failing to commit to a strategy

- Denying reality

- Avoiding making decisions

- Maintaining only comfort-zone networks, in which the leader is one of the "most expensive houses in their neighborhood"

- Tolerating low performers

- Needing to be liked

- Avoiding conflict

- Neglecting to listen enough

- Failing to maintain routines

- Tracking a few meaningful metrics

The prevalence—and problematic nature—of these habits is not just a matter of my observations; it's also supported by research. Leadership IQ, an online leadership training firm, surveyed more than one thousand board members from the private and public sectors who had fired their CEOs, to determine the most common reasons for termination. The top five responses?[7]

WHY CEOS WERE FIRED

MISMANAGING CHANGE — 31%

IGNORING CUSTOMERS — 28%

TOLERATING LOW PERFORMERS — 27%

DENYING REALITY — 23%

TOO MUCH TALK, NOT ENOUGH ACTION — 22%

0%   5%   10%   15%   20%   25%   30%

Source: Leadership IQ

You'll notice significant overlap between the Leadership IQ survey results and the unproductive habits listed above. They also share another commonality: *all* of them minimize action. The leaders who display these behaviors know what to do, and they know how to do it, but their unproductive habits render them unable to get things done—with dire consequences.

---

7   Mark Murphy, "Why the CEO Gets Fired (Change Management and More)," *Leadership IQ,* June 22, 2015, https://www.leadershipiq.com/blogs/ leadershipiq/35353153-why-the-ceo-gets-fired-change-management-and-more.

One of the mechanisms by which bad habits persist is explained by the Dunning-Kruger effect, a phenomenon discovered by social psychologists Justin Kruger and David Dunning. They found that people are likely to overestimate their abilities in a particular area, *especially* when they don't understand it very well.[8] Because they don't recognize their own ineptitude, they follow their own faulty logic without questioning it.

Dunning once shared an anecdote about psychiatrist Stephen Greenspan that demonstrates this phenomenon with epic irony. Greenspan, a widely admired expert on social competence, found out—two days after publishing a book on the subject of gullibility—that his financial advisor, the now infamous Bernie Madoff, had defrauded him of a large portion of his savings.[9] The fact that he was unfamiliar with financial matters paradoxically made him more likely to confidently invest with Madoff without doing the legwork to vet his decision.

We give just as much weight to our misconceptions as we do to our certainties. This prevents us from identifying and addressing unproductive habits and from seeking advice from those who are more experienced than we are—because we often don't realize we need the help.

The best way to counter this tendency is to be critical not only of information set before us but also of our ability to analyze it. The behaviors that constitute deliberate practice can help us do just that.

PRODUCTIVE LEADERSHIP HABITS

It's important to identify a handful of foundational habits that make leaders successful, and to implement deliberate practice to develop

---

8   J. Kruger and D. Dunning, "Unskilled and Unaware of It: How Difficulties in Recognizing One's Own Incompetence Lead to Inflated Self-Assessments," *Journal of Personality and Social Psychology* 77, no. 6 (1999): 1121–1134.

9   Olivia Goldhill, "The Person Who's Best at Lying to You Is You," *Quartz*, March 17, 2018, https://qz.com/1231534/the-person-whos-best-at-lying-to-you-is-you/.

them in yourself. Here are the top ten I've identified through my research and via direct observation in my coaching relationships.

- **Default to capitalize on luck:** As we discussed, addressing your thinking on luck—and choosing to capitalize on good or bad luck when you have it—will enable you to generate better returns. All of my clients have worked to embody this productive leadership habit through a combination of my coaching and reading Jim Collins's work. They grow to understand the value of generating a return on luck in all circumstances—not just with major events, like the loss of a large customer, and not just with negative events. With this in mind, they commit to capitalize on luck as a habit of thinking in response to both good- and bad-luck events.

  One seemingly minor, yet powerful example of how they successfully apply this concept occurs when a key member of the organization takes a temporary leave of absence, most often due to maternity, paternity, or protracted illness. Traditionally, business leaders see this situation as an unfortunate circumstance and, as such, choose to frame it as the "loss" of a key person for a period of time. They plan to accept the misery that will inevitably ensue during their teammate's absence, put a Band-Aid or two in place to hold things together, and count down the days until the individual's return.

  But those like my clients who have internalized the value of capitalizing on luck approach this type of situation differently. They think about the temporary loss as both an opportunity and a challenge, choosing to focus on how they can turn it into a boon for the business. A common return on luck solution here is to tap into existing staff to not only cover necessary responsibilities, but also reach the deliberate goal of helping other members of their team step up, stretch, learn, grow, and contribute in new and innovative ways. Everyone wins with this approach.

- **Be grateful:** When you appreciate and value what you have, you gain a clearer perspective. My clients are also extremely familiar with this habit, as I begin each of my meeting rhythms with a round of personal and professional appreciation. This ritual creates space for each executive to share and reflect on what they appreciate most and what's been working before we dig into the business at hand. It lightens the room and opens everyone to clearer thinking and increased collaboration.

- **Give—within limits:** Research shows that there are many advantages to being a giver. When you feel that you have information and resources to share, you cultivate an abundance mindset and reap the benefits that come with it. But as with anything, there are limits to the effectiveness of this habit. If you are giving away too much—think time and resources—you won't be able to stay on track and accomplish your own objectives. We'll explore this more deeply in chapter 7—How to Change Your Behavior.

- **Seek simplicity:** Many of us have been conditioned to favor complexity. For example, we tend to pay more for complicated things and services, imagining that they are more valuable. However, in an organizational setting, the exact opposite is true. Albert Einstein, one of the most sophisticated thinkers of the twentieth century, said, "The definition of genius is taking the complex and making it simple." Complexity won't scale.

- **Maintain a high question-to-statement ratio:** Most leaders I've encountered maintain a very low question-to-statement ratio. Their habit of thought is that they are experts, so they act accordingly and generally tell people what to do and how to do it. This might be useful in a very small start-up, when there is much to be accomplished by a small staff, but it's ultimately not scalable. Effective leaders ask many, many questions, empowering others to think, add new and different ideas, and identify their own weaknesses. My friend and colleague Keith uses a 20/80 rule of thumb here with his clients: the leader should spend 20 percent of his or her time asking questions and the remaining 80 percent listening to the answers. This practice multiplies effectiveness and is a powerful mechanism to motivate and grow the people on your team. You'll get others to help you do the thinking. They, in turn, will introduce new and different ideas, learn to spot their own weaknesses, and further develop the capacity of their own teams, perpetuating the cycle.

- **Believe that people are good; it's the process that's bad:** When something goes wrong, the default habit is to blame the people involved, rather than the process. But a bad or poorly communicated process can make even the most talented, dedicated staff look terrible. Unless you truly believe that people get out of bed in the morning thinking, "I can't wait to get to work today to screw things up," you need to reconfigure this habit. Question processes and communication first, before you interrogate the intentions, character, or capabilities of those involved.

  Research bolsters the importance of instituting this habit of thinking. In a study of the connection between individual trust and income levels, researchers found that trust was highly correlated to earnings, forming a bell curve. Those who put too little trust in others—as well as those who were overly trusting—had lower incomes, while those who demonstrated a slightly higher-than-average level of trust relative to the population (eight on a scale of zero to ten), had the highest incomes. Those who put the least trust in others demonstrated the poorest economic performance, an average of 14 percent lower than the highest earners.[10] As you can see, believing in your people literally pays off.

- **Practice good physical habits:** I won't harp here, because this is something you already know, but to be able to perform at the top of your game, sleep, exercise, and good nutrition are essential.

- **Have high expectations of others:** You've probably heard before that people will perform up to or down to the level of your expectations. If you think everyone's incompetent, then miraculously, they are. If you imagine them to be geniuses, you'll find that to be the case. Why? Your habit of thinking affects the way you treat others, and they respond accordingly.

  The data demonstrates that leaders who believe in the value of autonomy and individual responsibility and thus maintain an empowering leadership style eventually reap more benefits than their directive counterparts—those who simply tell their teams what to do. In a longitudinal study examining performance data from sixty teams, researchers found that teams run by directive leaders at first demonstrated better results. However, over time, groups led by those with empowering styles came out on top due to greater "team learning, coordination, empowerment, and mental model

---

10 Jeffrey Butler, Paola Giuliano, and Luigi Guiso, *The Right Amount of Trust*, National Bureau of Economic Research, 2009, Working Paper 15344.

development."[11] If you're looking to build something great over time, empowerment is key. Doing so requires that you maintain high expectations about the breadth and depth of your team's capabilities so that you are able to give them the space to achieve. As we'll see in chapter 6, high expectations are also an essential building block of accountability.

- **Maintain intentional focus:** We tend to multitask, attempting to work on as many projects as possible at once, hoping to move them all forward. Alas, countless research studies have exposed multitasking as ineffective and counterproductive. To make real progress, you must hold a small number of very important things in your mind and let go of the rest. This is a powerful fractal pattern that holds true at the individual, team, department, division, and overall corporate levels.

- **Overcommunicate:** We believe that everyone shares our framework of understanding and thought. We imagine that if we tell someone to do something once, we're done. But just because you've said it, that doesn't mean someone has understood you, that they have clarity on what they need to do, or that they actually know how to do it. Until your team is literally rolling their eyes and finishing your sentences, you haven't successfully communicated. Repetition is the mother of all learning—as we've seen through the power of deliberate practice—and the most critical element of habit formation. Well-executed huddles and weekly and monthly meetings are additional productive habits to reinforce the flow of information.

---

11 Natalia Lorinkova, Matthew Pearsall, and Henry Sims, "Examining the Differential Longitudinal Performance of Directive versus Empowering leadership in Teams," *Academy of Management Journal*, vol. 56. no. 2, accessed June 26, 2018, https://journals.aom.org/doi/abs/10.5465/amj.2011.0132.

My client David continues to experience the benefits of overcommunicating. David is the CEO of a virtual coaching firm that helps diabetics adhere to their medication regimens and achieve their health goals. Their diabetes clinical coaches are located throughout the United States, making his communication challenges substantially more difficult than those of a leader who has all of his or her team members under one roof. To better communicate with his staff, I suggested that David produce a ninety-second audio clip each week, in which he would discuss any significant events, updates, or hot topics that fit with the mission of his organization and that happened to be on his mind as CEO. I added that he could also use these recordings to single out employees or accomplishments that merit recognition throughout the company. The process would cost him approximately five minutes of his time per week and a total of zero dollars. He agreed to try it out.

After distributing his first recording, David received responses from multiple employees. The feedback was overwhelmingly positive—people shared that the messages made them feel truly connected to the company despite their disparate locations and that they were very grateful for the opportunity to hear from him. David's communications continually strengthen the virtual team's sense of connection and reinforce the spirit of teamwork, which is one of the firm's core values. To this day, about a year after the launch of his weekly recordings, David occasionally forwards me e-mails from his employees expressing gratitude for his updates. What may have seemed like overcommunication at first blush continues to garner appreciation from his staff. Most importantly, the business is more aligned than ever.

REFINING YOUR HABITS THROUGH DELIBERATE PRACTICE

In chapter 2 we discussed the virtues of deliberate practice—the habit that enables people to reach the top of their field. Researchers Ericsson, Krampe, and Tesch-Römer found that, rather than having the right teacher, the right opportunity, or raw, unbridled talent, it was top performers' motivation to stretch, to engage in extreme repetition, and to solicit a constant flow of feedback that made them great.

You'll notice that the core elements of deliberate practice are quite similar to the repetition and exposure that create habits. *When you engage the intentionality inherent in deliberate practice, you establish and maintain more productive leadership habits that will accelerate progress toward your aspirations.*

Let's say that, after reading the previous section, you decide that you want to change your unproductive leadership habit of not listening enough by improving your question-to-statement ratio. The first thing you could do is engage your leadership team in your effort, informing them of your goal and asking them to provide a flow of honest feedback on your progress. This feedback could include the creation of a signal to be used during meetings that—when issued—would indicate that it might be a good time to stop talking and start asking. Enlisting others to provide frequent feedback to help you stretch repeatedly will make a significant difference. Deliberate practice will improve your question-to-statement ratio—and any of the habits in the previous section, for that matter—generating tremendous returns.

Like the simple example detailed above, the following Activators and tools will help you modify your thinking and behavior, forming new, more productive habits that stick.

We are emotional beings. Unfortunately, our emotions don't reliably support our goals; rather, they tend to feed our egos, fears, and detrimental habits. One of the ways you can override emotion and interrupt some of your negative habits is to get as rational as possible. Here's an example of what this looks like in action:

Many CEOs are in the habit of being seduced by their own busyness. If this is the case for you, when you should be working on a big-picture (i.e., high-value) aspect of your business—like assessing trends or thinking strategically—you may be tempted to skip it in favor of fixing the thing right in front of you that seems to be broken.

Rather than give in to that urge, you can slow down and get rational. You can ask yourself, "How does missing the meeting serve me?" or you can compare the value of one activity to the other, weighing which has more the long-term payoff. You should also ask yourself whether someone else in the firm could handle the immediate issue, removing it from your agenda entirely and—perhaps—helping others learn and grow.

The flow of feedback integral to deliberate practice reinforces this Activator. Although posing these questions to yourself will provide insight, the most effective mechanism is to have someone else leading the inquiry. A coach, accountability partner, or mastermind group will challenge your thinking habits and help you avoid buying into faulty assumptions—like those promoted by the Dunning-Kruger effect.

The benefit of slowing down and getting rational recently became apparent to one of my longtime clients, a business that runs social athletic leagues for adults in cities across the United States. Internally, the company had been culture- and purpose-driven since its founding, but they struggled to infuse their mission into the external communities they were building. The WHY was missing from their messaging.

I knew that Simon Sinek's book *Start with Why* could help them crystallize their own WHY. Sinek urges people to determine their ultimate purpose and let that inspire everything that they do.12 Developing a WHY statement—an overarching proclamation that informs strategy, plans, and decision-making—and integrating it into every nook and cranny of their business would help them better operationalize their purpose and build the communities they envisioned.

But when I brought up the idea of creating a WHY statement, the executive team was resistant. Some felt that they had done this already; others felt it was unnecessary or just didn't see the point. One executive worried that it would feel manufactured or stilted.

The team's resistance was all habit. They were stuck in the wagon-wheel ruts of how things were in the past. To help them break their habit, I gave them an assignment to get rational. I asked them to explore the potential impact of what I was suggesting by watching Simon Sinek's TED Talk video about *Start with Why*. This wasn't a big request, but it was enough to help them get rational (and slow down).

By our next meeting, the team's thinking had shifted. They had become very open to the idea of creating a WHY statement, and several were already reading the book. They moved past their initial resistance and recognized the value of what I'd suggested. After much careful deliberation, the team finalized their WHY: "We believe that life is better when you have real personal connections, a caring community, and a sense of play."

Their WHY holds true today and has been fully integrated into the DNA of the company. Everything they say and do is consistent with their WHY.

By getting rational (and slowing down), the executive team

---

12 Simon Sinek, *Start with Why: How Great Leaders Inspire Everyone to Take Action* (New York: Penguin, 2011).

gained clarity and commitment to not only create their WHY but to do the things to make it stick throughout the organization. It's been ingrained in the company's fabric as their default habit of thinking.

TOOL: CHALLENGE YOUR ASSUMPTIONS

Now it's time to slow down, challenge your own assumptions and get rational. Complete the following exercise to isolate a particular problem and determine ways to get past it, breaking down the habits that reinforce your current thinking.

1. Write a statement about a business problem you are facing and why it exists, using *because* to link cause and effect. For example: growing our solutions business is difficult *because* our clients treat us like a vendor, not a partner.

   _____

   _____

   _____

   _____

2. Collaborate with a colleague to break down the challenge statement.

   a) What is the claim? This refers to the portion of the challenge statement after *because*—"our clients treat us like a vendor, not a partner," in the example above.

   _____

   _____

   _____

b) What evidence do you have to support this claim?

_____

_____

_____

c) Are there any assumptions involved here?

_____

_____

_____

3. Answer the following questions about the assumptions and evidence identified above.

   a) Do you agree with any of those assumptions?

_____

_____

_____

   b) Could the evidence behind your claim be invalid? If so, how?

_____

_____

_____

c) If the assumptions were proven false, how would you address this problem differently?

_____

_____

_____

4. List some ideas about how you can take action to address the problem.

_____

_____

_____

ACTIVATOR NUMBER 4

CHANGE UNPRODUCTIVE HABITS

Now that you've gotten rational and evaluated some of the assumptions that fuel your habits of thought, you can work to change your unproductive habits.

To begin, you must first recognize that all humans are creatures of habit and that our habits have helped us conserve energy and survive. But like most things, there are pros and cons to habits; we all have some that don't serve us, our relationships, and our aspirations.

Take the time to identify a few of your most unproductive habits. Not all of them—that could quite possibly become an unproductive habit in and of itself—but the ones that make a difference: the ones that are likely preventing you from reaching your personal and professional goals.

Remember the example of Ariel, the CEO who, as a child, was

conditioned to think that talking about money was inappropriate? If she maintains that habit of thinking into adulthood, changing it would require her first to recognize the habit, along with the ways in which it affects her decisions, choices, and actions in business.

DON'T RESIST, REPLACE

In addition to identifying her unproductive habit, Ariel must understand that there are *rewards* associated with her current pattern of thinking—if her habit weren't rewarding her in some way, she wouldn't maintain it. In her case, it's likely that by avoiding conversations about money, she avoids confronting her own discomfort with it or her fear that she isn't doing as well financially as her peers. But these "rewards" are small and short term.

Ariel must also explicitly identify the consequences of her habit. If she continues to hold financial matters at arm's length, she will never be able to achieve her long-term financial goals. Worse, she is likely to perpetuate her parents' example and raise children who are equally uncomfortable talking about money. Pinpointing the consequences of her unproductive habits and realizing that they far outweigh the rewards, in terms of long-term impact, help tip the scale toward change.

This tool will help you get rational with the unproductive habits you want to change, as well as the assembly of rewards and consequences associated with them. You will see that the "rewards" associated with the vast majority of your bad habits are short term, while their consequences are typically serious and abiding.

Once you've reviewed the rewards and consequences of each unproductive habit, it's time to find a replacement.

Why replace? Research has shown that replacement, rather than resistance, is the only way to permanently alter your habits for good. In a *New York Times* article titled "Resistance Is Futile. To Change

Habits, Try Replacement Instead," author Carl Richards describes ironic process theory, which dictates that when you try actively to change bad habits by resisting them, you are bound to fail.[13]

Richards demonstrates the theory in action by instructing his readers to "try *not* to picture a white bear."

Go ahead—try that on yourself right now. You simply cannot help but picture a white bear! The application of this is that your resistance to something forces it to occupy your mind, making it even more difficult to resist.

Richards offers a compelling solution: rather than resisting the habit, *replace* it. He shares the example of a friend who desperately wanted to break a particular habit. After unsuccessfully resisting it, he instead replaced it with something else, something very simple and totally innocuous: drinking a glass of water. Over time, his urge to engage in that particular habit lessened until he forgot about it entirely.

I overcame habits of thinking related to my relationship with money about ten years ago as a result of working with a coach. I was in the habit of charging everything on credit cards. Even though I paid them off every month, engaging in the habit meant I didn't have to interact with money on a daily basis.

My coach suggested that I begin carrying a hundred-dollar bill in my wallet at all times to replace my habit, which I do to this day. I don't take it out or pay for anything with it, but it reminds me that I have money in my pocket, which serves as the underpinning of my entire belief system about money.

---

13   Carl Richards, "Resistance Is Futile. To Change Habits, Try Replacement Instead," *New York Times*, March 19, 2018, https://mobile.nytimes.com/2018/03/19/your-money/resistance-is-futile-to-change-habits-try-replacement-instead.html.

TOOL: CHANGE YOUR HABITS

Use the template below to identify your unproductive habits and their consequences, as well as potential replacements and their positive impact.

CONSEQUENCES		POTENTIAL OUTCOMES	
REWARDS		**REWARDS**	
UNPRODUCTIVE HABITS		**PRODUCTIVE HABITS**	

1. List three unproductive habits.

2. What are the rewards that perpetuate those habits? Are they short term or long term?

3. What are the consequences of those unproductive habits?

4. List three productive habits that could serve as replacements.

5. What rewards will these productive habits provide? Are they short term or long term?

6. List some potential outcomes for replacing your unproductive habits, both in your business and in your life.

ACTIVATOR NUMBER 5  CHANGE YOUR NEIGHBORHOOD

Remember my grandpa Ben's advice never to buy the most expensive house in the neighborhood? It applies to relationships, too. If you find that you are one of the most expensive houses in your neighborhood, surrounded by people who don't stretch and challenge you—who reinforce your thinking and habits—you have to change your neighborhood.

My client Boris runs a company that makes porous metal filters and filter elements that are distributed worldwide for a multitude of applications. I recently offered him a seat at an exclusive two-day workshop for CEOs with Jim Collins. The workshop was costly and required a significant time commitment, including flying to Boulder, Colorado, where it was held. This experience was unlike anything Boris had done previously—it was the ultimate opportunity to change his neighborhood. He jumped at the chance.

Boris found himself in a roomful of CEOs from around the world—many of whom he considered to be a step up in terms of expertise and experience—not to mention Jim Collins himself.

He came back grateful and reenergized, with a slew of new ideas that are being implemented to advance the business.

When was the last time you changed your neighborhood? When was the last time you put yourself in a position that involved risking your ego or feeling intimidated by others in a room? When was the last time you upgraded your professional advisors, your coach, or your mentor? When was the last time you evaluated and upgraded your personal relationships, including where and how you spend time? That's what it takes to stretch, grow, and uncover the habits that may not be serving you.

TOOL: NEW NEIGHBORHOOD

Brainstorm a list of the ten people on the planet who are best positioned to help you learn, grow, plan, and execute in your business. List them by name, and be sure to include the name of their organization and the reason why they belong on your list.

Once your list is complete, begin the process of networking, using social media and direct outreach to make contact. As we learned back in chapter 2, what you focus on gains energy and grows in importance to you—a critical insight into this highly valuable tool. Connections to some people will be much easier than those to others; all will be worth the effort. Allocate a block of time each week to advance your progress toward a deliberate upgrade of your relationship neighborhood.

1. Name _____

   Organization _____

   Reason Why _____

2. Name _____

   Organization _____

   Reason Why _____

3. Name _____

   Organization _____

   Reason Why _____

4. Name _____

   Organization _____

   Reason Why _____

5. Name _____

   Organization _____

   Reason Why _____

6. Name _____

   Organization _____

   Reason Why _____

7. Name _____

   Organization _____

   Reason Why _____

8. Name _____

   Organization _____

   Reason Why _____

9. Name _____

   Organization _____

   Reason Why _____

10. Name _____

   Organization _____

   Reason Why _____

- Habits serve an important purpose in our lives: they save processing power and allow us to complete mindless functions while focusing attention on more pressing issues.

- Habits are formed through exposure and repetition. Once established, whether good or bad, they are hard to break.

- Mechanisms like the Dunning-Kruger effect, which states that people have the tendency to overestimate their capabilities in a particular area, especially when they don't know much about it, help perpetuate unproductive habits.

- The tenets of deliberate practice—repetition, motivation to stretch, and flow of feedback—will help you develop and maintain productive leadership habits that drive, rather than derail, your aspirations, purpose, and legacy.

- Slowing down, getting rational, and challenging your assumptions override emotion and interrupt unproductive habits.

- Identifying unproductive habits, the purpose they serve, and their corresponding rewards and consequences are the first steps toward creating change.

- To successfully terminate unproductive habits, you must replace rather than resist them.

- Changing your neighborhood by deliberately connecting to those who will help you advance lends valuable perspective and accelerates your progress.

CHAPTER 6

Beliefs

It was mid-morning on a sunny Saturday when the doorbell rang.

I opened the door and saw my neighbor Dennis, red in the face, jaw clenched tightly. We had always been friendly, but that morning he looked angry—ready for a fight.

"Hi, Dennis," I said, "How are you?"

"You know," he started, "Every day, your kids walk across my lawn to get to the school bus—back and forth, back and forth. They're wearing a path across it," he said animatedly, pointing to his front yard.

I followed his finger with my eyes. Sure enough, he was right. I saw the indentation in the grass my boys had trod as they made their daily round-trip trek to the bus stop.

"Wow—I see it. And I'm sorry. Thanks so much for bringing this to my attention," I told him. "From now on, I'll make sure they walk up and down our driveway. If this continues to be a problem, just let me know, and I'll handle it."

As I uttered those words, Dennis transformed right in front of my eyes. His obvious anger dissipated, his hands unclenched as he relaxed.

"Oh, thanks so much," he said, dropping the issue as he launched into a much friendlier conversation.

When he left, I wondered why he arrived the way he did. He must have experienced a similar situation in the past—and it apparently didn't go well. As Dennis approached my door that morning, he brought his past experience with him.

TIME PERSPECTIVES (PAST, PRESENT, AND FUTURE)

The way we conceptualize the past, present, and future informs our beliefs and the decisions, choices, and actions shaped by them. To get to the root of this reality—and our behavior—psychologist and Stanford professor emeritus Philip Zimbardo has conducted extensive research on the psychology of time. He discovered that each of us has a default setting—or time perspective—that determines how we view past, present, and future events.

PAST EVENTS

Individuals' perceptions about the past skew either toward the positive—meaning they tend to remember the past fondly, or toward the negative—making them more likely to retain bad memories.

You can easily observe this disposition in those around you. For example, imagine that two of your friends vacationed recently in Barcelona, Spain. When you ask them about their trip, the person with a past-positive orientation might tell you about the beautiful beaches and the perfect weather, while the one with the past-negative orientation will recall the terrible flight and an especially subpar meal.

Similarly, when facing a problem, a CEO with a past-positive orientation will likely recall past events to bolster their confidence as they approach the challenge. Meanwhile, a business leader with a past-negative orientation might approach the same situation with fear or dread, or he might choose to avoid it totally, remembering a similar past experience that didn't end well.

PRESENT EVENTS

Our conceptualizations of the present fall into two categories: present hedonism and present fatalism. Those who are present hedonistic live for the moment and do what feels good—to the point of recklessness, for those who demonstrate this quality in the extreme. While present hedonistic people sacrifice the future in search of enjoyment, those who demonstrate present fatalistic tendencies believe they can't control their fate—that the chips will fall where they may—and are therefore less likely to act to change their situation.

FUTURE EVENTS

Our outlook for the future is expressed in terms of high and low. Those with a high future time perspective are planners. They track. They're willing to delay gratification to accomplish their goals. Those with a low future time perspective take things as they come. They'll go for the easy thing now rather than holding out or tackling something hard for later rewards. They don't have the same level of discipline.

There are a number of factors that cause people to become more or less future-oriented. Living in a stable family, society, and nation fosters a high future orientation; when there is stability, your brain is free to plan ahead. Those with more education and future-oriented role models—factors frequently dictated by stability—often maintain the same values and usually end up more successful than their low future-oriented counterparts, in part because they are able to delay gratification.

Future-oriented people are also mindful of morality because they can understand the potential second- or even third-order impact of their actions.

FUTURE BELIEFS AFFECT PRESENT CHOICES

The work of Hal Hershfield, a psychologist at the UCLA Anderson School of Management, supports this assertion. To determine whether our conceptions of the future affect our present choices, Hershfield reviewed five studies on how people evaluate present and future rewards.

His findings were consistent: when people could envision their future, particularly in a positive fashion, they were more likely to make decisions and take actions with long-term payoffs. For example, one study explored the willingness of women and men aged eighteen to seventy-two to endorse unethical but profitable business decisions. Those who felt less connected to their future selves were more apt to tolerate unethical decisions.

This is another reason why the duality gap we discussed in chapter 1—between the leader you imagine you are and the one you aspire to be—is problematic: it demonstrates that the former is undeniably driving your bus and affecting your behavior accordingly, leading you to seek short-term rewards that ultimately thwart your purpose.

A high future orientation has its downsides too; sometimes your present pays the price. If you're extremely focused on working toward something with a long-term horizon—like building your business—it can be easy to sacrifice family, friends, and general enjoyment for an ever-extending timeline of achievement.

Another potential downside of high future orientation can be an inability to adapt. My future-oriented client Rob experienced this phenomenon while attempting to deepen his meditation practice. After a successful first experience attending a five-day meditation retreat relatively close to his New York City home, Rob decided to advance his practice further, registering for a completely silent five-day retreat at a highly regarded center in California. Excited to attend, he planned meticulously, scheduling time away from work, making travel arrangements, and packing for his trip.

Within an hour of his arrival, he began feeling deep disappointment that things were not as he'd expected. He'd envisioned a completely secular retreat yet found himself surrounded by the trappings of a Buddhist temple. He was required to hit a gong and bow before entering some of the rooms. His inner voice ran wild, and he questioned everything: the decision to take time from work, the cross-country travel to California, and why this was even happening to him. He desperately wanted things to be different, but he stayed with the program. On the third day, Rob saw things as they were and realized he had a problem with aversion—wanting things to be different than they were—not just at the retreat but also in his life. Rob's awareness of his inability to accept unmet expectations turned into his key learning from the retreat: he reduced his aversion by realizing how his imagination interacts with his perception of reality to generate highly emotional responses.

Rob was fortunate to overcome and learn from his inability to adapt. We can all benefit from his experience.

ACCEPT THE UNEXPECTED

Unexpected outcomes can be excellent sources of innovation and entrepreneurial opportunities, as the late management consultant, educator, and author Peter Drucker explained in his book *Innovation and Entrepreneurship*.

However, you have to be ready to seize these opportunities and generate the return on your good or bad luck, as we discussed in the previous chapter. If your time perspectives aren't balanced, it's easy to get frustrated and stuck—the way Rob did on his retreat. When you are unable to accept the unexpected, you lose the capacity to capitalize on unforeseen circumstances. In other words, as Louis Pasteur once said, "Chance favors the prepared mind."

So what does a prepared mind look like? Philip Zimbardo's research helped identify an ideal time perspective for achievement-oriented people:

- **High past positive:** You can clearly envision and remember past successes, helping you maintain a positive disposition and motivating you to pursue similar outcomes.

- **Moderately high present hedonism:** You are fully present but not so much that you ignore the future. And, importantly, you believe you have control over what happens in your life, driving you to go after the results you want.

- **Moderately high future orientation:** You are not too high, which could mean ignoring the present or becoming too much of a perfectionist; neither are you too low, unable to maintain the discipline necessary for long-term success.

To find out how your own time perspectives stack up, assess them online using the Zimbardo Time Perspective Inventory at http://www.thetimeparadox.com/zimbardo-time-perspective-inventory.

BELIEVE, AND YOU WILL ACHIEVE

Our thoughts about the future also play into achievement. Studies have repeatedly and reliably demonstrated that if you believe you can achieve something, you will work harder to make it happen. Moreover, if you believe in your team, they'll be more motivated to accomplish the goals you set. Why? As we discussed in the previous chapter, your expectations of yourself and others become self-fulfilling prophecies.

University of California psychologist Robert Rosenthal demonstrated the profound impact of expectations with an experiment on how teachers' expectations affect student achievement. At the beginning of the school year, Rosenthal selected children *at random* and informed their teachers that they had particularly high potential. At the end of the academic year, these "high-potential" children out-performed their peers.

The only explanation for their success was that their teachers believed they were especially talented, treated them accordingly, and the students met the challenge. This phenomenon goes both ways. If the teachers had been warned that the children selected were more difficult or less skilled than others, they would have lowered their expectations, and the students, in turn, probably, and unfortunately, would have met them.

THE NECESSITY OF ACCOUNTABILITY

Your expectations of others factor heavily into the accountability equation. To scale, you need to continually elevate and let go. Counting on others to handle increasingly important aspects of your business requires that you believe your team is capable of successfully executing.

Holding others highly accountable has proven difficult for every leader I've worked with, but if you believe those around you are able to step up to the challenge, you'll create an environment that will enable them to do so.

There are three non-negotiable building blocks to create accountability.

1. *Believe they are capable of completing the task or achieving the result you want.* This is essential. If you don't believe they can do it, they won't either. *I believe in you.*

2. *Tell them clearly why what you're asking of them matters.* Let them know it's important to you and exactly why that's the case. *This is important to me.*

3. *Show them repeatedly that you're watching.* Check in. Confirm their progress. Let them know you haven't forgotten. *I am watching.*

THE BUILDING BLOCKS OF ACCOUNTABILITY

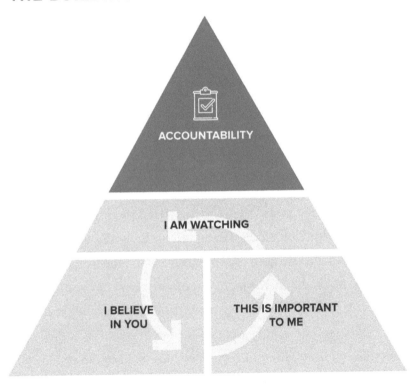

Every one of us—at some point in our lives—has engaged with a boss, mentor, or leader who helped us perform at our best. I encountered the best boss I ever had, Marion Suro, early in my career, when I was working at Alltel Information Services. Marion was a master at creating accountability. She had incredibly high expectations of me. She put me in a position to stretch, where I was continually challenged, and demonstrated that my efforts—and their outcomes—were not just important to her but to the region of the country she managed. She was also very deliberate in letting me know that she was always watching and that she expected that I would fulfill the commitments I made to her.

Often, as we passed each other in the hallway, she would cock her head to the side and say, "You're going to get that report to me by the end of business today, right?"

I could only reply with a confident "of course," before hustling back to my desk to ensure it was done and in to her before I went home that evening.

While it was maddening at the time, I know she made me better in so many ways and, in the process, helped me meet her high expectations and exceed my own.

OVERCOMING ANXIETY

Along with the inability to let go, anxiety plagues many business leaders—and reasonably so. Your role entails challenging conversations and high-stakes decisions on a daily basis. Plus, your livelihood, that of your team, and the well-being of your company all feel like they are in your hands. This anxiety can be further exacerbated by past-negative orientation, but there are useful techniques to address and channel it to arrive at more positive outcomes.

Harvard Business School professor Alison Wood Brooks first observed the impact of anxiety as an undergraduate student at Princeton. She was an a cappella singer, and during the audition process, she noticed that those who did well channeled their anxiety positively—into excitement rather than fear—while those who did poorly let their stress overtake their talents.

With this observation in mind, she surveyed two hundred people about what they would tell a coworker who was nervous about having to give a speech. The vast majority—90 percent—said they would tell the coworker to calm down, reassuring them that it would be okay.

Just under 8 percent of those surveyed would offer the seemingly better advice: encouraging their coworker to be excited rather than anxious.

There was a second part to her experiment. She had 113 people sing a song using a karaoke video game and told them that their singing would be scored. Participants were then divided into three groups. Prior to singing, the first group was instructed to repeat aloud, "I'm so anxious." The second was instructed to say, "I'm so excited." The third was instructed to say nothing.

The data corroborated her original observation as an undergraduate: those who said they were excited scored an average of 80 percent; those who said nothing scored 69 percent; and those who said they were anxious scored 53 percent.

Her findings have been replicated through multiple studies: those who talked about being excited immediately before a task significantly and consistently outperformed others.

The bottom line? As I relish telling my three sons all the time—*never in the history of calming down, did telling someone to calm down actually calm them down.* All that does is reinforce their anxiety. Rather, start channeling your anxiety into excitement.

Pause here for a moment and think ahead to a conversation, meeting, or event that is causing you some anxiety. Now reframe your feelings! By simply telling yourself repeatedly that you're excited to have a particular meeting or to connect with a potential customer, you will shift to a more effective state of mind.

ACTIVATOR NUMBER 6  MEASURE MORE

To be successful in any worthy endeavor, you must be willing to make trade-offs today for tomorrow's rewards. However, it's hard to focus on the future when your hair is on fire—which is often the scenario for leaders running high-growth firms. Forcing more future focus, and bringing ourselves closer to Philip Zimbardo's ideal, can help.

One way to do this is to measure more. Tracking progress on the path toward a larger objective helps you maintain present focus while also thinking long term. Here's an example:

My clients, the executive team at the leading online continuing education company for attorneys practicing in the United States, decided to implement an annual auto-renewal feature for customer subscriptions. Ideally, auto-renewal would keep more customers enrolled, thereby helping the business generate more revenue and more predictable results.

This undertaking required significant investment. There was also some risk involved in terms of client adoption—for example, would their customers be angry about this added feature? The inspiration-driven CEO David held the line, believing the benefits exceeded the risks involved.

There would be a one-year delay to future auto-renew revenue (their long-term goal) from the day each new customer subscribed, but in the meantime, the number of people who opted out of the program would be reported on a monthly basis. Just over a year later, the company is reaping the benefits of their enhanced future focus—and measuring more—with more retention and clearer numbers for next year.

Measuring more can help you reach your goals in business and beyond—I've used this Activator as a mechanism to reach personal objectives as well. For instance, several years ago, I decided to improve my health and fitness. In addition to weighing myself daily, I purchased a Fitbit and tracked my steps, as well as my daily calorie and water intake. I lost sixty-five pounds, changed a number of bad habits along the way, and am now more fit than at any other time in my life. Measuring these details on a regular basis was a powerful way to produce the overall outcome I desired.

TOOL: ACCOUNTABILITY CHART

To ensure that your long-term aspirations receive the attention, energy, and investment they deserve, you must build a habit of measuring more and increasing your future focus. Complete the Accountability tool and refer to it daily so that you and your executive team are consistently measuring and discussing progress toward your most significant aspirations. Add or modify roles as necessary, and update quarterly.

Similarly, identify your top one or two personal goals/priorities and itemize specifically how you will measure more to track your progress and remain fully accountable.

ROLE	NAME	THIS QUARTER	THIS YEAR	WITHIN 3 YEARS
				MOST IMPORTANT METRIC, RESULT, OR OUTCOME:
CEO	*David*	*Employee NPS*	*% of "A" Performers*	Double Net Profit
CEO				
COO				
CFO				
Sales				
Marketing				
Operations				

| | | MOST IMPORTANT METRIC, RESULT, OR OUTCOME: | | |
ROLE	NAME	THIS QUARTER	THIS YEAR	WITHIN 3 YEARS
HR				
Technology				

PERSONAL GOALS/PRIORITIES	MOST IMPORTANT TRACKING METRIC/ ACTION		
Lose 25 pounds	*Log daily food & drink consumption into a calorie-tracking app*		

ACTIVATOR NUMBER 7  LEVERAGE YOUR PAST

There are no facts embedded in any of your memories. All of our recollections are literally stories that we tell ourselves. This is why people in the same place at the same time remember things differently. When you recognize this, you can reframe the way you tell these recalled stories—to yourself and to others—and thus alter your perspective on your past.

David Rendall realized the value of shifting perspective when he began his career. As a child, David exhibited classic symptoms of Attention Deficit Disorder (ADD). He couldn't sit still in class. He got in trouble all the time. As he likes to say, he was every school administrator's worst nightmare. Though very smart, David grew up with the notion that his ADD was a weakness, and that it would prevent him from achieving any real success in life—a belief that was continually reinforced by most of his teachers and school administrators.

When he eventually entered the business world, he struggled. His troublesome traits from childhood were a liability there as well.

One day, he realized that, while these traits were making him unhappy in an office setting, they made him well suited for public speaking. That's exactly what he decided to pursue. As he thought about his own story and began researching how others overcame their ADD, he concluded that our greatest weaknesses can also be our greatest strengths—a reality he documented in his book *The Freak Factor* and shares as a highly regarded speaker, with engagements around the world.

To transform your thinking about the past, you can ask questions to reframe your own story.

- What if you're wrong about a particular belief you have about yourself?

- What was the good that came from a bad prior experience?

- Are there alternative explanations for events or different ways to look at what happened in your past?

These shifts can be the key to your future success.

TOOL: REFRAME YOUR PAST

Think of a time in your past—an experience, a particular year or age, or perhaps a multiyear period that you remember more negatively than positively. With that time period in mind, answer the following:

List one to three significant negative outcomes and/or events you experienced during that time.

1. _____

_____

2. _____

_____

3. _____

_____

What did you learn and/or what positives can be taken from these events?

_____

_____

_____

_____

_____

_____

_____

List one to three positive events you experienced during that same time.

1. _____

_____

2. _____

_____

3. _____

_____

How did these events—both negative and positive—improve your life to date?

_____

_____

_____

_____

_____

_____

How can these events—both negative and positive—improve your future?

_____

_____

_____

Repeat this exercise as often as necessary to reframe and more productively leverage your past.

ACTIVATOR NUMBER 8  ENJOY THE JOURNEY

Philip Zimbardo and others have repeatedly demonstrated that moderate present hedonism—being in the moment—is a valuable trait. I experienced this firsthand at a recent conference in St. Louis. I serve on the Global Advisory team of Gravitas Impact Premium Coaches (formerly Gazelles International), a leading global coaching organization and the conference host.

At 7:15 a.m. on day one of the event, my phone rang. It was one of my colleagues, who was scheduled to lead a sales training session that morning. He was stuck in Chicago due to bad weather and wouldn't be able to teach the class, slotted to begin in forty-five minutes, at 8:00 a.m. Eighteen coaches representing six continents would be waiting to learn about selling skills and techniques from this elite sales coach.

"Mark," he said, "I'm not going to make it. I need you to teach my class this morning."

Teaching that class was the furthest thing from my mind—I hadn't even showered yet! But now I didn't have a choice. I realized

I had facilitated the sales development presentation once before, in Berlin the previous May. I found my PowerPoint slides and facilitation guide from the session, jumped in the shower, bounded out of my room, and—heart racing—made it to the classroom at eight o'clock on the dot.

That morning with the coaches was fantastic; their survey scores demonstrated that they had gotten a tremendous amount from the session—and so did I. Instead of resisting the situation in front of me, I chose to go with the flow, to accept the unexpected, and teach that class. In the end, I had an opportunity to make an impact on those coaches and to learn from them as well.

Life is full of unexpected situations. If you can be okay with that reality, you can learn to capitalize on it and hopefully enjoy the journey along the way.

In any unexpected situation, ask yourself the following questions:

- What is the opportunity here?

- How can I capitalize on, learn from, or grow from this moment?

- How can I use this experience to help others?

- What am I giving up or losing out on by choosing not to enjoy the journey right now?

TOOL: SCHEDULE THE PRESENT

We often spend our emotional and physical energy focused on the past (what's already happened) or on the future (what we want to or think will happen) at the expense of the present—the moment that's right here, right now. Use this tool to make commitments and schedule more spontaneous, present moment–focused activities to enjoy the journey.

EXAMPLES OF PRESENT-ORIENTED ACTIVITIES

- Pick a direction—north, south, east, or west—and go for a drive without a destination in mind.

- Set aside a full weekend day without any plans. Decide what to do that morning.

- Take two or three employees to lunch and get to know them personally; don't talk about work.

- Go to a comedy club. Even better, practice telling jokes to others.

- Listen to live jazz music.

- Pick a day and choose to say yes to almost everything.

- Get a massage.

- Practice relaxation exercises or meditate.

- Allocate one hour to wander around the office and get to know people personally.

- Ask someone else to select your meal at a restaurant.

- Go for a hike and enjoy nature.

- Sing.

- Spend time with others who are fun-loving and spontaneous rather than planners.

- Leave your wristwatch at home.

- Make up a new game with a young child.

- Take a very long, very hot shower.

- Pick a favorite childhood activity—perhaps flying a kite or blowing bubbles—and do it.

- Talk to strangers.

- Play a game and lose on purpose.

- Go to a playground, swing, slide, and play.

- Ride a roller coaster or do something else that scares you.

- Learn a new skill.

- Create a work of art.

- Ask someone else in the room to run one of your meetings.

- Go dancing or take a dance lesson.

- Flip a coin or use a random number generator to make a decision.

- Go to a psychic, just for fun.

1. Pick one or two items from the above list (or create/find additional ideas to pursue) that you are choosing to do in the next seven to ten days.

2. Communicate the choices to your significant other, a friend, or a colleague, coach, or mentor, and ask for help planning the activity and/or holding you accountable, if necessary.

3. Schedule the activity in your calendar.

Repeat this exercise weekly to schedule the present and enjoy the journey.

- Developed by psychologist Philip Zimbardo, time perspectives describe our general attitudes about past, present, and future events.

- Your beliefs about time—and your past and future self—inform how you behave. They affect what happens in the present. You can use these factors to address accountability and anxiety in yourself and in others.

- By measuring your progress, you can make choices and take action that will make you more likely to accomplish goals.

- Memories are not factually based. Rather, they are stories we tell ourselves. You can positively leverage past experiences by reframing the stories you tell yourself and re-envisioning your weaknesses as potential strengths.

- If you can go with the flow—embrace the unexpected—you can capitalize on it.

Master Your Inner Voices

CHAPTER 7

How to Change Your Behavior

Now that we've illuminated the growth-killing impact of your motivators, habits, beliefs, and the eight Activators to help you overcome them, we can dive deeper into how to change your behavior.

We'll get into three mastery tools in just a bit, but first, let's touch on some mechanisms of behavioral change that will help you get unstuck—no matter what issue you're addressing. These methods can be applied to all the Activators and tools we've already covered, as well as to those we'll introduce next.

YOU'RE EXACTLY WHERE YOU WANT TO BE

We'll start with this harsh-sounding but crucial insight: *wherever you happen to be in any area of your life—work performance, wellness, relationships, or anything else—you've chosen to be exactly there.* If you want to alter a particular circumstance, such as working too hard for too little return, you must first understand that your current situation is of your own design.

Every day, you make choices—some huge, some minuscule, and everything in between—and it's taken millions, if not billions of them to bring you to where you are right now. Each time you made a choice, you did so to achieve something you wanted at the time. The problem is, while making many of those choices, you were distracted by the short-term rewards. You didn't contemplate the long-term consequences.

Imagine this scenario: An employee asks you how to complete a particular task. You're working on something else, it's nearing the end of the day, and you begin to think about the effort behind their request. You might rationalize that explaining how to do it could take thirty minutes, he'll still probably get it wrong, and you'll have to spend even more time to correct it. But if you just do it yourself, it will only take five minutes. You tell him not to worry about it; you'll take care of it for him. You make the choice.

That's what you want in the moment—to save time, get it done, and get it done right. Thousands of choices later, you are in your current position: you're working fourteen hours a day handling minutiae for others because time after time, teaching someone else seemed unreasonable.

Luckily, as we've already uncovered, we have the ability to consciously choose to delay gratification for long-term gain—you've surely seen the benefits of making all kinds of sacrifices to grow your business. But the next, more frustrating reality is that we are genetically programmed to choose the short-term reward. We have the power to say no to that second piece of chocolate cake when we're trying to lose weight, but we're also wired to want it.

But when you understand both your propensity to choose instant gratification and your power to defer it and when you understand that you are right where you've chosen to be, you can start thinking differently about your behaviors and taking steps to change.

The following practices work to address behaviors that aren't serving you. You don't have to use them in any particular order, or even try them all. Instead, choose one or two and put them to the test. For guidance on identifying behaviors to change, refer to the assessments in the appendix and to the list of productive leadership habits in chapter 5.

THINK YOUR WAY INTO BEING

There are two ways to change your behavior: you can either "think your way into being" or you can "be your way into thinking."

If you choose to address a behavior via thinking, over time, with significant mental effort, you'll begin to behave differently. For instance, if it's difficult for you to deliver direct feedback to your team, finding ways to change your thinking about the issue could be your first step in tackling it. You could change your neighborhood and surround yourself with business leaders who are awesome at delivering feedback. You could read a book on how to effectively offer constructive criticism, or you could develop a set of affirmations to assure yourself that you can do it—and repeat them three times a day. The idea here is that if you think about something for long enough, eventually it will seep into your being and lead you to change your behavior.

TOOL: AFFIRMATIONS

Affirmations can be a powerful tool. They are built on the premise that your mind doesn't know the difference between what is real and what is imagined. For example, suppose it's late at night, and you're alone in your house. You hear a creak downstairs. You *imagine* that it must be a prowler.

Are you any less frightened than if you *know* with certainty that a prowler is there? No. *Imagining* the situation evokes just as much fear. Affirmations build confidence to overcome the invented thoughts and scenarios that hold us back. You can develop a set of targeted affirmations to address specific behaviors you wish to change.

Affirmation statements should have the following qualities:

- They should be positive.

- They should be in first-person singular, present tense.

- They should promote high expectations of yourself and your capacity but also be realistic.

- They should directly relate to your commitments or goals.

Here are some examples of affirmations. Try them on for size. If they feel good, use them; if not, create your own. Write them down on three-by-five cards and place them in locations where you spend a great deal of time (in your office, your car, on the bathroom mirror, etc.), and carry them with you. Plan to read them aloud three times a day, and develop a schedule to do so (first thing in the morning, immediately after lunch or just before you leave the office, and right before you go to sleep, for instance). They are a great way to keep your attitude positive, your mind on your goals, and your thinking aligned with your aspirations.

EXAMPLES OF AFFIRMATIONS

- I am a master communicator.

- I lead by example.

- I set daily goals and achieve them.

- I ask questions to bring out the best in others.

- I am a results-oriented leader.

- I am genuinely concerned about helping my employees grow and evolve.

- I am the master of my emotions. When I feel fear, I plunge ahead.

- I play to win.
- I bring positive energy to every situation.

BE YOUR WAY INTO THINKING

While thinking your way into being is a valid route, it requires the luxury of time and the discipline to do the work (i.e., deliberate practice). Unfortunately, that time requirement renders this method less than ideal for most of the CEOs I know, who need to get things done.

Fortunately, there's another, faster way: *being* your way into thinking, colloquially expressed as "fake it till you make it." With this technique, if you want to have more direct conversations with your team, you would emulate the desired behavior right away, until it becomes natural.

To start, you could reach out to a friend or colleague who is great at giving feedback, and ask her about what she does in those moments when one of her direct reports needs a course correction. You might inquire about what she's thinking when she walks through the door, or how she opens up the conversation once they're sitting down.

Perhaps you worry in these situations that you'll ruin someone's day, while your friend is thinking, "I'm about to do this person a great service because, without this feedback on their performance, they wouldn't have the opportunity to get better and reach their potential." It's the same situation, the same conversation, but with two very different beliefs driving—and thus determining—the behavior.

But then, instead of just thinking about her insights via affirmation, you would imitate her behaviors immediately. It will feel pretty uncomfortable at the beginning, but you'll learn from the process. Over time, it becomes more comfortable and creates a tangible impact on the way you think and act.

Neurological research backs this up. In one experiment, psychologists had people either smile or frown before completing an emotional survey. Those forced to smile scored better than those forced to frown before evaluating their mood—even though the only difference between the two groups was their pre-survey action.

Often, the best way to modify a behavior is just to do it—to jump in—though our fears often get in the way. I see this repeatedly with the new coaches I mentor. They'll complete their training and return to their home offices ready to establish their coaching practices. But then they'll spend a week rereading all the manuals, sharpening their pencils, and putting their office supplies in order. They'll spend another month working on their website, making sure their voicemail is just so, and ordering business cards with their new logos. The one thing they won't do? Pick up the phone and contact a potential client.

They believe that when they get all their ducks in a row, when they know the material inside and out, when they feel like the professionals they hope to become, they'll be able to make the call. But all their efforts are just delaying the process. The way to really learn—and learn quickly—is to dial the first number on your list and say hello.

Educational theorist David Kolb's experiential learning theory also underscores the power of being your way into thinking. According to Kolb's theory, all learning occurs through the following four-stage cycle:

- Concrete experience: You do or encounter something new.

- Reflective observation: You consider any inconsistencies between your previous understanding of a concept and insights brought on by that new experience.

- Abstract conceptualization: You come up with new ideas or revise previous considerations based on the experience and your reflection on it.

- Active experimentation: You test out strategies and evaluate the results.

Learning only takes place when all four stages of the cycle occur. As such, the "doing" portion of being your way into thinking—Kolb's active experimentation element in the cycle—is an essential ingredient. It's how you learned to walk, to ride a bike, to be a parent, and to run your company. It's also how you'll become a better business leader.

Several years ago, I worked with a leadership team that struggled to embody their own core values. This is a relatively common problem. It's easy to understand and accept core values on a sheet of paper. It's easy to point out someone in the organization who recently demonstrated a core value in a daily huddle. It can even be relatively easy to fire a subordinate for failing to uphold your values. It's much harder to tap a peer or your boss on the shoulder and tell her you saw her violate a core value. For this team, it was the proverbial elephant in the room. Everybody was breaking the organization's core values, and no one was talking about it.

Meanwhile, they were attempting to think their way into being, imagining that if they just immersed themselves in the philosophy behind their core values, those values would soon be assimilated. But they didn't have the time or discipline for daily affirmations, and it wasn't working very well. As such, they needed to start *doing*—to *be* their way into thinking—by calling themselves and each other out when they violated their own core values. Changing their modus operandi would have been a much faster and more effective way to achieve their desired end. Unfortunately, this CEO and his team were unable to change and align their own behaviors with the core values they defined for the organization.

The team made it through three components of Kolb's learning cycle but was unwilling and/or unable to complete the fourth and most important element: the doing. After several months of stagnation, I ended my coaching relationship with them. As I mentioned in chapter 4, I exit relationships that lack accountable execution so that I can help others who are willing to do the work required (via deliberate practice), maximizing my impact and honoring my life's purpose.

IF/WHEN, THEN

In 2001, three German researchers, Brandstatter, Langselder, and Gollwitzer, conducted a fascinating study on influencing behavior. They asked people housed in a drug rehab facility to prepare résumés to be used after their release. They were divided into two groups. One group—the control—was asked to draft their résumés by the end of the day; they weren't given any further instruction. The second group was asked to make a plan to complete them by formulating an "if/when, then" statement. An "if/when, then" statement names a cue and the behavior it will provoke. For this group, it went as follows: "*When* I finish my lunch today and clear my table space, *then* I will begin to work on my résumé."

The results were astounding. None of the members of the control group finished their résumés. The same day, 80 percent of the "if/when, then" group completed theirs. The statement itself had an enormous impact on the outcome.

An "if/when, then" plan is far superior to a simple intention. Why?

It prepares us to notice the cue. The group agreed in advance to what they were going to do (complete their résumés) and specifically when they were going to do it (after they finished their lunches).

Human behavior is governed by a rule of consistency—we behave in a manner that aligns with our conception of ourselves. If someone prompts you to ponder your own magnanimity by asking whether you imagine yourself to be a generous person, and your phone rings moments later, and someone asks you to support a worthy charity, you're more likely to donate than someone who wasn't primed in such a manner.

Similarly, if you tell yourself you'll work on your résumé when you finish your lunch, the rule of consistency dictates that, in order to maintain consistency—which you are naturally inclined to do—you'll follow through.

There's a lot of power in that little statement, and I use it to address all kinds of issues in my coaching practice. For instance, I've worked with many CEOs who were not classically trained in accounting and finance. In many cases, though they ran a successful business, they remained overwhelmed by the numbers. Their fears often drove them to avoid financial information and reports—creating active ignorance and further reinforcing the problem.

To change this behavior, you could use an "if/when, then" statement: "*When* I receive our monthly financials, *then* I will sit down that day for a minimum of thirty minutes to understand them." While this statement itself won't turn you into a CFO or a finance whiz overnight, it will cue you to do the thing you are avoiding. And that's exactly the point.

The "if/when, then" format can be used to create deliberate cues to encourage good habits. For instance, as CEO, when someone asks you a question, you are probably inclined to offer an answer. But turning a question around and asking what *they* think could generate new ideas, create space for others to contribute, and foster more independent thinking throughout your organization.

Defaulting to respond to a question with a question, rather than with an answer, is a highly productive leadership habit. To build this habit, you could create an "if/when, then" cue, something like, "If

I'm asked a question, then I will respond with a question to gather more information." This cue effectively ups your question-to-statement ratio and makes room for your team members to tap into more of their potential.

RELATE, REPEAT, AND REFRAME

In his book *Change or Die*, business and technology writer Alan Deutschman explores the reasons why change is so hard. His analysis brings to light three key insights:

RELATE: To change, you need to believe that change is possible. Cultivate relationships with those who can help you see that whatever it is you're trying to do is attainable. As a coach, I am a significant part of this "relate" component for my clients, because I help leaders see and believe in the possibilities in front of them. I do this by sharing stories of other clients who have accomplished something similar or by pointing out the elements of their team and organization that can help them advance.

Partners, mentors, role models, coaches, and peer groups can supply the relatability factor necessary for change. Remember my grandpa Ben's dictum, however (don't be the most expensive house in the neighborhood), and make sure the people you're drawing on have the "next-level" experience and knowledge to help your progress, rather than hinder it.

REPEAT: As we discussed in the Habits chapter, we learn through repetition. Once you've identified the change you want, test out the new behavior or thought pattern. Then seek out feedback from others. Repeat the learning process, get guidance, encouragement, and direction along the way, and repeat again. Sound familiar? This is deliberate practice in action.

REFRAME: To transform a new behavior into a new way of being, your thinking needs to change as well. When I started my health and fitness journey, I had to reframe the way I thought about exercise, which had never been something I enjoyed. By choosing activities I liked—hiking and long walks through the neighborhood with my wife to get started, and now invigorating sessions at a kickboxing gym—I successfully integrated it into my life. Today I genuinely look forward to working out.

KNOW WHEN TO SAY NO

In his book *Give and Take*, psychologist, author, and Wharton professor Adam Grant illuminates his research findings on the impact of "giving" and "taking" behaviors in business. He found that in a business environment, both the highest and lowest performers are givers. A confusing outcome—one would expect it to be one way or the other.

Perhaps the highest performers are those with the most to give, or maybe it's their generosity that has made them so successful. On the other hand, those who give too much may end up being the lowest performers, because their tendency to sacrifice attention, time, and resources for others causes them to neglect their own jobs. How could it be both ways?

When Grant and his team dug into the results, they found that the high-performing givers knew when to say no. The low performers did not—to the point where it damaged their own performance.

Most CEOs I know rightly consider themselves to be givers. They think they need to give in order to build the organizations they want—which they do. But as we discussed in chapter 4, their yes-to-no ratios are often inverted from the ideal. Why? They simply don't know when, how, or why to say no.

The propensity to give—and give without limits—also ties into our fears of ego, scarcity, and failure. It's a mechanism by which many of us justify our importance (ego) or further exacerbate fears that if we don't handle things personally, the business won't perform properly—or might even fail entirely.

Knowing when to say no honors your priorities and protects the value of your time. How do you know when to say no?

If you're surrounded by takers (and you should know them when you see them), it's not only time to start saying no, but also to ask yourself whether you have the right people on the bus. Alternatively, if—as a giver—you are creating dependence that prevents your people from learning and growing to benefit the business, say no now.

As with all things, there are more and less effective ways to say no. Researchers have investigated this topic, too, and you can use their insights to do a better job of saying no and getting the message through. For instance, New York University professor of marketing Adam Alter found that saying *don't* is far more effective than saying *can't*. Why?

Don't is empowering—it indicates that you've made the choice to do something yourself, rather than bowing to external forces, which *can't* indicates (and no one likes being controlled).

In his book *Irresistible: The Rise of Addictive Technology and the Business of Keeping Us Hooked*, Adam references a study in which women attempted to achieve an exercise goal. Those who said, "I can't miss a workout," stuck to their commitment 10 percent of the time, while those who said, "I don't miss a workout," completed their exercise routine 80 percent of the time.

Start simple. Tell yourself, "I don't take on tasks that can be done by others," or "I don't commit to things that don't serve my ultimate goals," and watch your yes-to-no ratio transform for the better.

Think of it this way: If you were a parent who picked up your toddler every time she reached for you, she'd never learn to walk. Humans learn from doing, not just from thinking about stuff. You didn't learn to ride a bike by reading a book about it. You had to get on the bike, fall off, and get back on again. Changing your behavior is the same. It often takes multiple tries with multiple models, but starting and actually doing something is the first step.

Where must you *choose* to say no so that you are able to say yes to honoring a commitment?

Once you've identified areas where you can say no, take it to the next level by tracking your yes-to-no ratio and capitalizing on the power of Activator Number 6: Measure More.

GOOD ENOUGH IS GOOD ENOUGH

"For many events, roughly 80 percent of the effects come from 20 percent of the causes." With that brilliant statement, Italian engineer, economist, sociologist, and philosopher Vilfredo Pareto gave us the gift of the 80/20 Rule.

At its core, it's about big and small: 20 percent of your customers—typically the most difficult ones—are causing 80 percent of your customer service expense; 20 percent of the résumés that come through represent 80 percent of the value of the marketplace, and so on.

The 80/20 Rule also applies to perfectionism—the majority of the value in any endeavor often comes from a relatively small amount of the overall effort. And yet, perfectionism frequently limits our progress and fuels our three big fears—scarcity, ego, and failure. When we feel compelled to get it exactly right before we make a decision, render an opinion, or have a conversation with someone, our desire for perfection amplifies our perception of risk, and, of course, those fears that are already in our way. We fool ourselves into thinking there's more at stake than there actually is.

In business, very few things need to be perfect, and in most situations—like having a conversation, writing a memo, making a plan, and even changing your behaviors and habits—the drive for perfection doesn't deliver any marginal return. If you can keep the 80/20 Rule in mind, and remember that good enough is usually *plenty* good enough, you can reduce your fears and accomplish more.

HOLD YOURSELF ACCOUNTABLE

In his book *Triggers*, business educator and coach Marshall Goldsmith explores the power of leveraging accountability to get things done. The mechanisms Goldsmith employs highlight the power of measuring more. He suggests asking yourself a set of self-assessment questions on a daily basis to evaluate whether you are doing your best to accomplish your goals. For instance, if you are attempting to change your question-to-statement ratio, you may ask yourself, "Did I do my best to shift my question-to-statement ratio today?" Inquiring as to whether you are doing your best will elicit qualitative rather than quantitative responses, adding more meaning to the numbers-driven data you may be collecting. To make this even more effective, add an accountability partner to the mix, someone you can check in with frequently regarding your progress.

Goldsmith uses these strategies himself. Each day, he asks himself a set of twenty-one questions to determine whether he is making progress toward his ambitions. He also has his own accountability partner, someone he speaks with for five minutes a day, every day, regardless of where in the world he is or what he is doing.14 These are fantastic ways to make sure your choices align with and honor your commitments.

---

14 Marshall Goldsmith and Mark Reiter, *Triggers: Creating Behavior That Lasts—Becoming the Person You Want to Be* (New York: Penguin Random House, 2015).

They also help you focus on the things that matter to you and—as you know—where focus goes, energy and attention flow. Ultimately, only you can hold yourself accountable. Creating a multipronged plan to drive your own dedication to your goals will highlight their importance and enable you to put in the work to get there.

REVISIT THE CHANGE YOUR HABITS TOOL

Research on behavior concretely connects behaviors, habits, the rewards that perpetuate behaviors, and the long-term benefits of replacing unproductive habits with something more beneficial. This is an opportune time to revisit the Change Your Habits tool in chapter 5 and evaluate your behaviors. Use this to identify unproductive behaviors you'd like to change as well as the replacement behaviors that will better serve your aspirations.

- You are exactly where you want to be. Your current station in any area of your life is a product of the numerous decisions and choices you've made and the actions you've taken up until this point. To make any real change, you must understand this.

- You can either "think your way into being"—a route that requires significant time and discipline—or you can "be your way into thinking," a faster, more uncomfortable, yet effective path. Seek out examples of the behaviors you want to employ and emulate them—fake it until you make it— until they begin to feel natural.

- "If/when, then" statements are powerful influencers of actions. They cue behavior to help honor your commitments.

- Relate, repeat, and reframe is a three-step approach to behavioral change. It requires you to seek others who can support your efforts, to repeat the behavior you wish to adopt and learn throughout the process (deliberate practice), and to reframe your thinking to make the changes stick.

- Be a giver, but know when to say no and track your yes-to-no ratio. It's the only way to protect your time, energy, and focus as a leader. Use the word *don't* instead of *can't* to indicate that your no really means no.

- Good enough is good enough! Use the 80/20 Rule, or Pareto Principle—that a relatively small amount of anything is responsible for a disproportionately large amount of the results—to focus on what matters rather than getting caught up in the details and pursuing perfection.

- Hold yourself accountable with strategies that require you to evaluate your progress and focus on the importance of your goals.

- Use the Change Your Habits tool located in chapter 5 to replace less desirable behaviors/habits with new ones better aligned with your aspirations.

CHAPTER 8

Putting It Together

The insights and tools in this chapter employ everything we've discussed so far—the research, narrative, stories, and all eight Activators—to help you get more of what you want and less of what you don't.

Before we get started, let's quickly recap the Activators:

REDUCE FEAR

ENJOY THE JOURNEY

INCREASE INSPIRATION

THINK COMMIT LEARN ACT

LEVERAGE YOUR PAST

GET RATIONAL (AND SLOW DOWN)

MEASURE MORE

CHANGE UNPRODUCTIVE HABITS

CHANGE YOUR NEIGHBORHOOD

1. **REDUCE FEAR**

Fear is at the root of many decisions; it unconsciously drives your thinking and behavior and limits you in the process. But when you choose to confront fear, you can overcome it. There are a number of techniques and tools to prevent fear-based decision-making, including slowing your thinking, changing your neighborhood, and explicitly naming what you're afraid of.

2. **INCREASE INSPIRATION**

Increasing inspiration is analogous to the process of reducing fear—and it's equally important. When you believe in what you're doing and where you're headed, you raise your inspiration. Inspiration outweighs fear only in a two-to-one or greater ratio, the ratio necessary to act. Knowing your WHY, evaluating your yes-to-no ratio, and ensuring that your decisions, choices, and actions are self-directed are valuable ways to both increase inspiration and stay on track.

3. **GET RATIONAL (AND SLOW DOWN)**

One of the ways to override emotion and interrupt your negative habits is to get as rational as possible. Taking the time to question and explore your urge to make a particular decision, choice, or action can help. The flow of feedback integral to deliberate practice also reinforces this Activator, but remember: while posing these questions to yourself will provide insight, the most effective line of questioning is external—an experienced coach, accountability partner, or trusted peer will provide the truly objective perspective you need.

4.  CHANGE UNPRODUCTIVE HABITS

We all have habits, particularly habits of thinking, that don't serve us. Unproductive habits persist because we weigh short-term rewards much more heavily than long-term consequences. Replacing them requires longer-term, not shorter-term thinking. Productive leadership habits include the following:

- Capitalizing on luck—either bad or good
- Seeking simplicity
- Maintaining a high question-to-statement ratio
- Having high expectations of others
- Overcommunicating

5.  CHANGE YOUR NEIGHBORHOOD

If you find that you're the most expensive house in your neighborhood (i.e., you're surrounded by people who don't actively challenge you), then it's time to change your neighborhood. Doing so isn't easy: No longer being one of the smartest or most accomplished in the group may be threatening to your ego. Accepting this potential discomfort is necessary to stretch yourself, to uncover habits and behaviors that aren't serving you, and to grow.

6. MEASURE MORE

Tracking granular, even daily progress on the path toward a larger objective—whether personal or professional—helps you maintain present focus and enables you to more clearly determine next steps on the path to longer-term goals.

7. LEVERAGE YOUR PAST

Our recollections are actually just stories that we tell ourselves. When you recognize this, you can reframe the way you tell these recalled stories—to yourself and others—and thus alter your perspective on your past. These shifts are key to productive, present-moment decisions, choices, and actions.

8.  ENJOY THE JOURNEY

Life is full of the unexpected. If you can be okay with that reality, you can learn to capitalize on it and enjoy the process. In any unexpected situation, ask yourself these questions:

- What is the opportunity here?

- How can I capitalize on this moment or learn from it?

- How can I use this experience to help others?

The tools we've covered in the previous chapters are narrowly focused, each employing a particular Activator to help you progress. But the three tools that follow are much broader, incorporating multiple Activators and research-backed techniques for maximum impact.

As a reminder, you can access these—and all the tools and assessments presented in this book—at www.activators.biz.

CLARITY OF PURPOSE—A DEEPER DIVE

I've never met a CEO who didn't think he or she already had clarity of purpose, but most haven't been through the rigorous process necessary to truly unearth the reason they're here.

As a result, when asked what they believe their purpose to be, they usually offer a relatively surface-level answer—something like "I want to build a great company," or "I hope to create an amazing environment for my employees." They may state that their overarching goal is to make their customers happy or to provide their kids with every opportunity in life. While those are all valuable aspirations, the truth is that none of them gets to the heart of the matter.

Why go deeper?

Research has shown us that we have a strong affinity for concepts bigger than ourselves. Think back to a peak experience in your life—perhaps you completed a significant project for an organization you cared about or fulfilled a meaningful commitment. Whatever that experience was, it probably allowed you to contribute to or be recognized by a cause or group that mattered to you. Having a strong, clearly defined purpose allows you to take advantage of this human desire—to feel like you are part of something greater than yourself—without needing an external group or a cause. You will be able to regulate your own inspiration as a result and operate from a powerful internal locus of control.

Throughout each day, I maintain awareness of my purpose: to unlock human potential. That awareness helps me act when I don't want to. My purpose drives me to do the hard things and relish life's high points in a deeper way. While it certainly fuels my business, it transcends it, by far: my purpose is about how I want to be remembered. It's about my own legacy that I can choose to build each day.

That's what the Life's Purpose tool helps you do: determine how you'll build your legacy one day at a time.

A strong sense of purpose will increase inspiration and encourage you to take action when it could be tempting to give up or back down. Your purpose will also drive your decisions and choices, ensuring that they align with your longest-term aspirations.

TOOL: LIFE'S PURPOSE

Give yourself one week for every step in the process that follows, thinking deeply about each one:

STEP 1: Take eight sheets of paper. At the top of each sheet, write one of the following eight categories:

- Mental/Learning

- Social

- Physical

- Financial (material)

- Family

- Business/Career

- Spiritual

- Other (for items that do not cleanly fit in one of the categories above)

For each category, ask yourself, "What do I want?" List *everything* you can think of—things big, small, long term, short term, tangible, intangible, realistic, unrealistic, et cetera. Do *not* list the same item in more than one category.

Alternate listing your entries at the top and bottom of each page so that they eventually meet in the middle.

STEP 2: Hold a forced-choice "competition" within each category to determine the item most important to you (picture the seeding of teams or players in a tournament, where winners advance to the next round).

1. Start at the top of each page and work your way down (do not alternate top and bottom for this; instead compare the first two items on your list, followed by the second two, and so on). You must eliminate a want in each round in favor of the item you'd rather have. Continue until you determine a winner for each category.

2. Take your eight categories and list them in alphabetical order, from Business/Career to Spiritual.

3. Run a "finals" competition among all the categories to determine your number-one want.

STEP 3: Build your ideal "on purpose" day.

1. List the same eight categories on the left side of a sheet of paper.

2. Write down the number of hours you would like to be awake on an imaginary ideal day (typically twelve to eighteen hours, depending on the individual).

3. Using the number of hours you're awake, create a time budget for your ideal day. Allocate a number of hours to each of the eight categories. For instance, how many hours do you want to spend with your family? How many do you want to spend

working on your business? Remember, you are budgeting for an *ideal* day—however you choose to define it—rather than a typical one.

4. At the top of a second sheet of paper, write "My Ideal On-Purpose Day." Along the left side, write your ideal wake-up time at the top and your bedtime at the bottom (this should encompass the total number of hours you plan to be awake). Then fill in thirty-minute increments, so the page looks like a day planner.

5. Schedule your day based on the categories you budgeted for on the previous sheet. For example, if you wake up at 7:00 a.m., you may block the first hour of the day for Physical. Maybe the next two hours are dedicated to Mental/Learning. Continue with this process until the time you budgeted for each category has been scheduled.

6. Now swap the category names for your top want in each category. For example, if your top want in the Physical category is "Live to 100," then the time block from 7:00 a.m. to 8:00 a.m. should now read, "Live to 100." This might seem a bit odd at first, but it indicates that you should be spending that hour working toward your ultimate desire, whatever it may be.

7. Compare your ideal "on-purpose" day to a typical one. Consider the differences and why they exist.

STEP 4: Draft your Life's Purpose Statement.
1. Consider your eight most important wants. If you had trouble winnowing the list down to just eight, you can also evaluate the runners-up, those that "lost" in the last round of competition (making sixteen items in total).

2. Taking into account your top wants, create a Life's Purpose Statement using the following format:

"I exist to serve by _____ing _____."

(For example, my Life's Purpose Statement is "I exist to serve by unlocking human potential.")

3. Try this purpose statement on for size during the week. Set aside specific times each day—say, 10:00 a.m., 2:00 p.m., and 8:00 p.m.—to pause and ask yourself, "Am I *on* purpose or *off* purpose?"

If you're *on purpose*, how does that feel? Why?

If you're *off purpose*, how does that feel? Why?

Continue to work this step until your purpose statement resonates deeply. One common sign that you're on the right track is getting goosebumps when you speak your Life's Purpose Statement out loud.

Here's to a purposeful life!

GET THINGS DONE

While the Life's Purpose tool addresses your inspiration from an existential, big-picture point of view, the Action tool is designed to be used for the tactical situations you encounter on a daily or weekly basis. It is a practical, actionable tool that will help you get things done—particularly things you are avoiding or struggling with. It answers and resolves the driving question behind this book: *what is it that I'm not doing, but know I should?*

The Action tool can be used to address any number of issues that require action—something to be done—right now. This powerful tool will help you and your team generate the impetus to act, whether you need to have a hard conversation with your second-largest customer, to communicate more transparently with your staff, to become more comfortable with your financials, to fire a toxic high-performer, or to do anything else you're avoiding.

As you use the Action tool, you will notice that it employs a number of familiar concepts from the book. You'll begin by naming your duality gap—the difference between who you think you are and who you want to be—and then changing your neighborhood, being your way into thinking, and capitalizing on the impact of "if/when, then" cues.

TOOL: ACTION

Answer the following questions and prompts:

1. What action are you avoiding, struggling with, or hesitant to execute?

    _____

    _____

_____

_____

2. Identify your duality gap.

   a) Describe how you actually feel as you think about and/
      or try to take action. Be descriptive and use emotional
      language.

   _____

   _____

   _____

   _____

   b) Describe how you ideally envision yourself feeling as you
      think about and/or try to take action.

   _____

   _____

   _____

   _____

   c) Circle one or two key descriptive words in each of the
      above responses.

   _____

   _____

   _____

   _____

3. Name three people you know who embody your ideal aspiration.

_____

_____

_____

4. Think about those three people specifically. List the beliefs and behaviors that enable them to take action when others would delay or avoid it. Ask them if you are unsure!

_____

_____

_____

_____

_____

_____

_____

5. Pick one behavior and create an "if/when, then" cue for yourself.
Behavior:

_____

_____

_____

"If/when, then" cue:

_____

_____

_____

6. Choose a simple, yet meaningful reward you can give yourself each time you execute the target action.

_____

_____

_____

7. Share your action and "if/when, then" cue with someone who has no stake in your outcome, like a coach, mentor, forum mate, or peer. Ask for their help and support. Take action!

CLARIFY YOUR THINKING

Although relatively infrequent, big strategic decisions weigh heavily on us due to perceived high stakes, risks, and irreversibility. Maybe you're trying to decide whether to abandon a particular product or service you're currently offering. Maybe you're thinking about committing to a new strategy, a different customer segment, or a new business partnership that will open up some previously unavailable capability. Or you may need to commit to retooling or modernizing your factory. These higher-stakes commitments demand a different approach to clarifying your thinking by ensuring that the hidden growth killers don't render you unable to think critically.

The Commitment tool requires some investment to complete properly, but given what's at stake—and the inevitable tendency of your mind to interrupt the rational thinking process—it's well worth the effort.

Just like the Action tool, the Commitment tool employs multiple Activators and several of the behavioral techniques outlined earlier. You'll notice that the Fear Reduction process plays a big part in the effectiveness of this tool: as you evaluate any major commitment, it's crucial to be open and honest about what you're afraid of. In addition, you must consider the long-term potential value of the commitment to increase inspiration and get rational (and slow down) as you think it through.

Remember these models depicting how we *think* leadership works, versus how it *actually* works?

HOW LEADERSHIP ACTUALLY WORKS

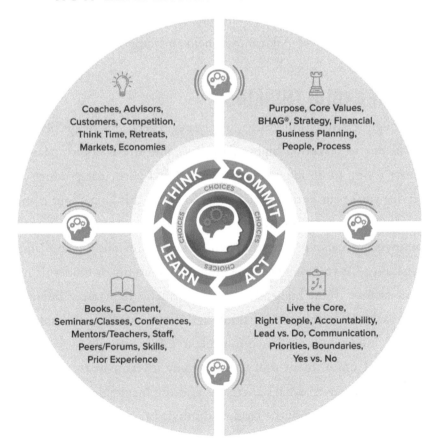

This tool will help clarify your thinking and prevent your inner voice from getting in the way.

TOOL: COMMITMENT

1. Name a commitment you are struggling with or hesitant to make. _____

_____

_____

2. Identify your fear concerning the commitment as it applies to the following categories:

Scarcity _____

_____

_____

_____

Ego _____

_____

_____

_____

Failure _____

_____

_____

_____

3. Identify your inspiration—the WHY. Be visionary and specific. What are the potential benefits, gains, or advancements driving this particular commitment? What might expand or grow as a result of making it?

_____

_____

_____

_____

_____

_____

_____

_____

4. Work the Fear Reduction process (< F).

   Pinpoint your fears. Be as specific as possible. Identify the worst-case scenario outcome if you make a commitment.

_____

_____

_____

_____

_____

Is this a temporary or permanent condition? Are the potential negative outcomes temporary or permanent?

_____

_____

_____

_____

Estimate the *realistic* probability (expressed as a percent) of this outcome.

_____

Name specific previous experiences you've had that support your assessment of the permanence and probability of the worst-case outcome.

_____

_____

_____

_____

_____

_____

_____

_____

In the event of your worst-case outcome, how would you recover? Be specific here as well.

_____

_____

_____

_____

_____

_____

_____

_____

_____

Name one to three risk areas associated with your commitment. Indicate your perception of the current risk profile on a continuum. Examples:

Price   high risk -----X------------------------- low risk

Testing   more risk -----------------------X------- less risk

_____   ------------------------------

_____   ------------------------------

_____   ------------------------------

How can you reduce the perceived risks associated with your commitment?

_____

_____

_____

_____

_____

Discuss the Fear Reduction information above with someone who has no stake in your commitment, like a coach, mentor, forum mate, or peer. Invite them to challenge your thinking.

5. Engage in the Inspiration Improvement process (2I > F).

Write a detailed description of the best possible outcome. Include both potential short- and long-term gains. Make it vivid.

_____

_____

_____

_____

_____

_____

_____

_____

Explain how this best-case outcome supports your life's purpose and/or other important major life aspirations:

_____

_____

_____

_____

Name others who succeeded after making a similar commitment:

_____

_____

_____

_____

_____

Name specific previous experiences and examples of *your* success that affirm and support your ability to attain a positive outcome:

_____

_____

_____

_____

_____

6. Work steps 4 and 5 until you feel like the magnitude of the inspiration for your commitment is at least twice the magnitude of your fear: $2I > F$. Use *logic* to evaluate your fear and *emotion* to evaluate your inspiration.

7. Reevaluate the commitment, and if applicable, describe the next action you'll take to move forward.

_____

_____

_____

_____

_____

Now that we've put the pieces together and you've seen how the Activators, tools, and techniques work in concert to address most issues you encounter, your real-world application and mastery of your inner voice is about to begin. In the next and final chapter, we'll talk about personal growth, the application of deliberate practice techniques, happiness, and how to forge your own path forward, bolstered by what you've learned here.

- The Life's Purpose, Action, and Commitment tools combine Activators and other insights we've covered throughout the book to deliver long-lasting, high-impact results.

- When you uncover your true purpose, you feel as if you are part of something greater than yourself—without needing an external group or a cause.

- A strong sense of purpose, which you can identify using the Life's Purpose tool, will increase inspiration, effectively drive your decisions and choices, and encourage you to take the right action.

- The Action tool answers and resolves the driving question behind this book: *what is it that I'm not doing, but know I should?* It addresses tactical issues—the kind you encounter on a daily or weekly basis.

- Just like the Action tool, the Commitment tool amalgamates Activators and several of the behavioral techniques outlined in previous chapters. As you evaluate any major commitment, it's crucial to be open and honest about your fears, to consider the long-term potential value of the commitment to increase inspiration, and to get rational (and slow down) as you think it through.

- The Commitment tool requires an investment of time to complete properly, but given what's at stake—and the inevitable tendency of your mind to interrupt the rational thinking process—it's well worth the effort.

CHAPTER 9

We Gather Strength as We Go

The application of brute force is neither sustainable nor scalable. If you still believe that you can maintain your leadership status quo by muscling your way through the obstacles you encounter, at some point, you'll be subjected to a harsh reality check. Even if you can't see the myriad ways in which your behavior is limiting you, eventually the flawed decisions, choices, and actions will come back to bite you in a big way, as leadership coach Marshall Goldsmith explains in his 2007 book, *What Got You Here Won't Get You There.*

Goldsmith's thesis is that the habits and behaviors that may have contributed to your leadership success in the past don't necessarily serve you now. That idea also applies to your business overall and your ability to drive future accomplishments and results. Advancing further requires reevaluating and altering your approach, both organizationally *and* as an individual.

As I stated in chapter 1, *I have never observed a business in which the sustained growth rate of the company exceeded the personal growth rate of the people running it.* Your own individual progress is absolutely essential to your company's success. For guidance regarding where growth would help you the most, complete the self-assessments in the appendix, or visit www.activators.biz to download them. They'll create clarity regarding where you have the most to gain, as well as identify which of the eight Activators you need to amplify to accelerate your progress.

The Life's Purpose, Action, and Commitment tools presented in the previous chapter combine multiple Activators with research-backed methods to help you overcome the hidden growth killers and change your thinking and behavior. Here, in conclusion, we'll take it to the next level once more, by covering methods to holistically implement the tools we've discussed in all corners of your life.

By reinforcing these now-familiar concepts once again, we'll ensure that you understand the multitude of ways in which they can be combined for maximum impact.

At this point, you have a clear sense of how your personal leadership model is affected by the hidden growth killers—your motivators, habits, and beliefs—and you know what they cost you in terms of your ability to effectively think, commit, act, and learn. Use the following figure to visually refresh your understanding of how these unconscious factors interrupt your progress and hinder your success.

HOW LEADERSHIP ACTUALLY WORKS

Below is a complete list of the Activators, so that you can refer back to them—all in one place—whenever necessary.

1. Reduce Fear

2. Increase Inspiration

3. Get Rational (and Slow Down)

4. Change Unproductive Habits

5. Change Your Neighborhood

6. Measure More

7. Leverage Your Past

8. Enjoy the Journey

If you're playing to win (and you should be), remember that you're running a marathon, not a sprint. Your path to victory will never be a straight shot, nor will you prevail in every footrace along the way. Rather, you'll take two steps forward and one step back, another step back and three steps forward. But over time—through all those fits and starts—if you deploy what you've learned here, you'll dramatically improve your odds of eventually emerging triumphant.

At times, you will wonder if it's really worth the price—the work involved, the energy it takes to retool your plans, and the imperative to do hard things. But when the things that matter to you most—your purpose, freedom, abundance, and legacy—are at stake, you'll find whatever you need within yourself to persist.

UNCOVER YOUR LIFE'S PURPOSE

In the previous chapter, we discussed the importance of identifying your life's purpose and using it to successfully drive your decisions, choices, and actions. Knowing your purpose—whether it applies to a particular circumstance or result or to the entirety of your existence—has a remarkable impact on your ability to overcome adversity and achieve the outcomes you desire. The tools in this book provide multiple opportunities to dig deeply into the powerful potential of purpose.

Complete the Know Your WHY tool in chapter 4. Name a specific outcome—a goal, target, belief, habit, or behavior that you want to change—and ask a series of repetitive questions to fully establish the WHY behind the desired change. Doing so will help you identify the most meaningful benefits and enable you to cultivate enough inspiration to act.

Next, move to the Life's Purpose tool in chapter 8. Your purpose statement should be goosebump-inducing. It should move you. As such, it should act not only as a force multiplier for your inspiration but also as a guiding principle for all that you think and do.

THINK BIG, START SMALL, BE STEADY

Now that the big picture is clear, pick one Activator to begin. Use a corresponding tool to break the ice, as well as the techniques outlined in chapter 7: How to Change Your Behavior:

- Think your way into being

- Be your way into thinking

- Create an "if/when, then" statement

- Relate, repeat, and reframe

- Rely on the 80/20 Rule to banish unnecessary perfectionism

- Turn your time- and energy-sucking yesses into nos.

Don't forget the Change Your Habits tool in chapter 5. Use this tool to understand the rewards and consequences associated with unproductive habits and then find effective replacements that help them stick.

Finally, recruit one or more people—perhaps your entire executive team—to support you in these change processes. You might just inspire them to consider how their hidden growth killers affect them, both personally and professionally.

DELIBERATE PRACTICE— GATHER STRENGTH AS YOU GO

We've returned to the concept of deliberate practice on numerous occasions throughout this book because the research-backed trifecta of stretching, repetition, and continuous feedback is incredibly effective to create mastery in any domain.

But nothing worthwhile is completely free of effort, or even of discomfort. Whether it's your ego or another factor that must be challenged along the path, the discomfort that arises is essential to continually advance—and you'll be that much more resilient for it.

Similar to the mechanisms that make deliberate practice work, both the Action and Commitment tools require discipline, analysis, and a willingness to stretch in order to be effective. I encourage you to keep a copy of the Action and Commitment tools handy at all times. Actively seek out situations in which to use them. Those that will benefit from the Action tool will arise more frequently, as they should.

Consider creating an "if/when, then" statement that cues you to use the tools—perhaps something like "*When* I feel a duality gap—a disparity between how I feel in a particular moment and the way I imagine my ideal self—*then* I'll use the Action or Commitment tool to clarify my thinking."

No matter how deliberate you are or how well you employ the ideas in this book, inevitably, you're going to screw up. You're going to have setbacks. You'll do and think the wrong things—everyone does. Remain purposeful and take it in stride—we're only human, after all. In the marathon you're running to battle the unconscious forces that hold you back, your willingness to do the work and stick with it are what really matter.

ENGAGE YOUR TEAM

It's not just you. The hidden growth killers operate in each of us to suboptimize decisions, choices, and actions, compounding the costs for your entire company. Of course, the Activators and tools you've put to work to tackle your own inner voice will help your team too.

As you clarify the unconscious forces that affect your decisions, choices, and actions, invite your executive team to join you. Help them identify, analyze, and work to change *their* motivations, habits, and beliefs, if they haven't already. Don't hesitate to share what you've learned and to find ways to incorporate some of the Activators and tools into your firm's processes.

ENJOY THE JOURNEY

Even as you're doing the work, dealing with serious issues and facing the periodic seemingly insurmountable challenges, there is always room for Activator Number 8: Enjoy the Journey.

Research shows that gratitude and happiness are vital to personal and professional success. In reviewing numerous scientific studies, gratitude expert and UC Davis professor of psychology Robert Emmons found a "wide array of psychological, physical, and relational benefits associated with gratitude."[15] And gratitude didn't just improve outcomes for the individuals expressing it: family, friends,

---

15   Robert Emmons, "Queen of the Virtues? Gratitude as a Human Strength," Reflective Practice: Formation and Supervision in Ministry: 51, http://journals.sfu.ca/rpfs/index.php/rpfs/article/view/59/58.

and colleagues reported that their grateful counterparts "are more pleasant to be around . . . more helpful, more outgoing, more optimistic, and more trustworthy."[16]

Gratitude also enhances self-esteem, as a 2014 study found.[17] Researchers Lung Hung Chen and Chia-Huei Wu discovered that athletes with grateful dispositions demonstrated higher levels of self-esteem than less thankful players. Higher self-esteem promotes clearer thinking and better performance, making gratitude valuable for everyone. Those who are grateful are also able to better identify opportunities, and thus create—even from the ashes of a defeat— more return on luck, as we discussed in chapter 5.

Stopping to smell the roses is a popular cliché for a good reason. Take a moment to consider all that you've accomplished so far, as well as the personal and professional aspects of your life that bring you joy. Think of those who have made it possible for you to be who you are and where you are today and of how much you've learned along the way. Keep that mentality as you continue your journey. Your body, mind, and business will thank you—and, as the research demonstrates, you should thank them right back.

WITH OUR THOUGHTS, WE MAKE OUR WORLD

A number of years ago, I was on a business trip to Boston. I needed to eat an early dinner before my next meeting, and I noticed a Chinese restaurant near my hotel. It was the most convenient option, so I headed in.

At the end of my meal, quite predictably, I received a fortune cookie. I dutifully removed the plastic wrapper, cracked the cookie

---

16   Emmons: 55, http://journals.sfu.ca/rpfs/index.php/rpfs/article/view/59/58.
17   Lung Hung Chen and Chia-Huei Wu, "Gratitude Enhances Change in Athletes' Self-Esteem: The Moderating Role of Trust in Coach," *Journal of Applied Sport Psychology*, 26:3 (2014): 349–362, DOI: 10.1080/10413200.2014.889255.

open, and then marveled at what I was reading.

I still have that fortune. It reads, "With our thoughts, we make our world."

I know this to be true. Now, so do you.

You know what to do, you know how to do it, and you now know *why* it's so difficult to execute what you already know you should be doing. But armed with the eight Activators, tools, and research-based tactics to guide you, you'll be able to think more clearly, get more done, and accelerate toward your aspirations.

You can close the duality gap between the leader you think you are and the leader you envision yourself becoming. You're probably closer than you think.

As you continue your journey down the road less traveled, following in the footsteps of other highly successful leaders—and making a few footprints of your own—I wish you the very best. Freedom, a meaningful legacy, and abundance await, and you already have everything you need to get there.

APPENDIX

The appendix contains two self-assessments that you can use to evaluate where you are now, as well as the Activators and tools that will be most effective to help you get where you want to go. As a reminder, these self-assessments and all the tools contained in the book are available for free download at www.activators.biz.

TOOLS

For quick reference, here are all the tools we've covered, and where they can be found within the book:

HIDDEN GROWTH KILLER SELF-ASSESSMENT

Determine whether you do the following items often or rarely, and check the corresponding box. Move quickly through the list and try not to overthink these—go with your first impulse.

	Often	Rarely
1. I commit to and stick with a business strategy.		
2. I boldly articulate my vision.		
3. I hold on to a clear sense of purpose.		
4. I make decisions swiftly and with ease.		
5. I actively seek data and information that inform me of "bad news."		
6. I communicate transparently and frequently with all employees.		
7. I consistently make time for deep interactions with our customers.		
8. I continually upgrade my network with higher quality individuals.		
9. I critically evaluate my professional advisor relationships.		
10. I leave peer groups/forums when they cease to be effective for me.		
11. I protect time weekly for strategic/higher-level thinking.		

	Often	Rarely
12. I act swiftly to coach or remove low-performing employees.		
13. I keep my commitments.		
14. I hold others highly accountable to their commitments.		
15. I hire people who are smarter/more capable than I am.		
16. My leadership team and I engage in regular, consistent planning.		
17. My leadership team and I consistently track and use metrics.		
18. 18. I am comfortable with and regularly engage with our financials.		
19. I downgrade my optimism when evidence to support it is lacking.		
20. I delegate frequently and effectively.		
21. I live all of our core values.		
22. I maintain effective boundaries with clients and staff.		
23. My desire to be respected is greater than my desire to be liked.		
24. I create clear priorities and honor them in my choices and scheduling.		

	Often	Rarely
25. I implement the things I learn from books, conferences, peer groups, etc.		
26. I actively encourage constructive disagreement and debate.		
27. My organization uses outside professionals to help implement things we've never done before.		
28. I deliver honest, negative and/or constructive feedback to my staff.		
29. We raise our prices.		
30. I solicit advice only from those who are qualified and credible regarding the matter at hand.		
31. I focus on the big picture and avoid too much detail.		
32. My direct reports would characterize me as an effective coach.		
33. I share my own vulnerabilities with others.		
34. When I am wrong, I admit it.		
35. I keep focus on the primary task at hand without distraction.		
36. I actively address interpersonal conflict.		
37. I listen more than I speak.		

	Often	Rarely
38. I create contingency plans to manage known risks and hedge against unknown outcomes.		
39. I delegate broadly and fairly, balancing others' workloads.		
40. I maintain a disciplined daily schedule and follow routines.		
41. I think of others first when solving challenges and evaluating opportunities.		
42. I maintain an even temper and have good self-control.		
43. I am tactful and avoid over-sharing sensitive or personal information.		
44. I operate outside of my comfort zone.		
45. I take good care of myself physically and mentally.		
46. My staff would describe me as humble.		
47. I willingly compromise when necessary.		
48. I think about positive past events in my life much more frequently than negative ones.		
49. I correlate achievement, not busyness, with productivity.		
50. Others would describe me as impulsive, fun-loving, and adventurous.		

Determine the total number of marks in the RARELY column. This number demonstrates the impact of hidden growth killers on your effectiveness as a leader:

- Fewer than 10: Some impact

- 11–25: Moderate impact

- 26–50: Significant impact

Based on the outcome of this assessment, consider which Activators and tools could be most effective for you, and begin to implement them in your work and life. The Activators Self-Assessment can help provide clarity as well, enabling you to reflect on your strengths and weaknesses, as well as the Activators that correlate to any issues you're having.

ACTIVATORS SELF-ASSESSMENT

On a scale of 0 (low) to 10 (high), rate yourself on each of the following questions.

Activator	Rating
1. **Reduce Fear:** How effective are you at quieting the voice in your head and reducing the impact of your fears?	
2. **Increase Inspiration:** How good are you at being purpose-driven and using inspiration as a tool to motivate yourself and your team?	
3. **Get Rational (and Slow Down):** How skilled are you at employing deliberate, rational thinking rather than a more rapid, emotionally driven approach?	
4. **Change Unproductive Habits:** How effective are you at identifying and permanently changing behavioral and thinking habits that don't serve you?	
5. **Change Your Neighborhood:** How disciplined are you about upgrading the quality of the people—advisors, peer groups, mentors, etc.—surrounding you?	
6. **Measure More:** How good are you at creating and tracking clear, highly visible metrics that reinforce progress toward your long-term aspirations?	
7. **Leverage Your Past:** How effective are you at framing past experiences—even the bumps, bruises, and biggest setbacks—as positives to propel you forward?	
8. **Enjoy the Journey:** How good are you at fully experiencing your life—with joy and spontaneity—in the present moment?	

WHEEL OF CLEAR THINKING

Each spoke of the wheel on the next page correlates to an Activator. Plot your self-assessment rating for each Activator on its corresponding spoke, where a score of 10 is on the farthest point from the hub, and a score of 0 is at the center. Then connect the dots to see the shape of your wheel. Notice where any dips or bumps occur.

What is the number-one Activator you need to master?

_____

_____

Why? _____

_____

_____

_____

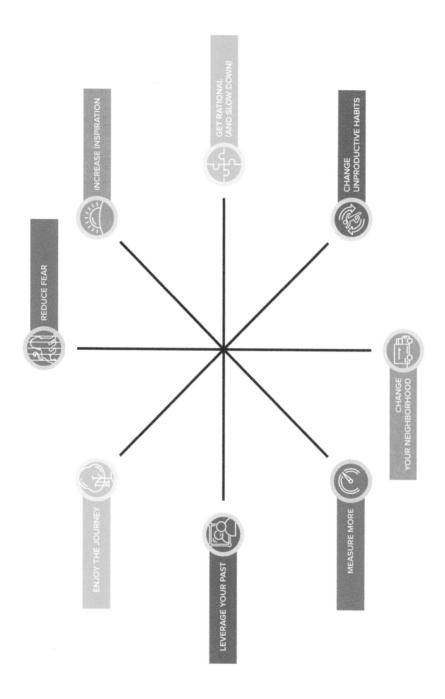

GET RATIONAL
(AND SLOW DOWN)

INCREASE INSPIRATION

CHANGE
UNPRODUCTIVE HABITS

REDUCE FEAR

CHANGE
YOUR NEIGHBORHOOD

ENJOY THE JOURNEY

LEVERAGE YOUR PAST

MEASURE MORE

CPSIA information can be obtained
at www.ICGtesting.com
Printed in the USA
LVHW081825311018
595217LV00017B/17/P